The Thing

G. K. Chesterton

The Thing

G. K. Chesterton

1929

CONTENTS

INTRODUCTION

IT will be naturally objected to the publication of these papers that they are ephemeral and that they are controversial. In other words, the normal critic will at once dismiss them as too frivolous and dislike them as too serious. The rather one-sided truce of good taste, touching all religious matters, which prevailed until a short time ago, has now given place to a rather one-sided war. But the truce can still be invoked, as such terrorism of taste generally is invoked, against the minority. We all know the dear old Conservative colonel who swears himself red in the face that he is not going to talk politics, but that damning to hell all those bloody blasted Socialists is not politics. We all have a kindly feeling for the dear old lady, living at Bath or Cheltenham, who would not dream of talking uncharitably about anybody, but who does certainly think the Dissenters are too dreadful or that Irish servants are really impossible. It is in the spirit of these two very admirable persons that the controversy is now conducted in the Press on behalf of a Progressive Faith and a Broad and Brotherly Religion. So long as the writer employs vast and universal gestures of fellowship and hospitality to all those who are ready to abandon their religious beliefs, he is allowed to be as rude as he likes to all those who venture to retain them. The Dean of St. Paul's permits himself genially to call the Catholic Church a treacherous and bloody corporation; Mr. H. G. Wells is allowed to compare the Blessed Trinity to an undignified dance; the Bishop of Birmingham to compare the Blessed Sacrament to a barbarous blood-feast. It is felt that phrases like these cannot ruffle that human peace and harmony which all such humanitarians desire; there is nothing in THESE expressions that could possibly interfere with brotherhood and the sympathy that is the bond of society. We may be sure of this, for we have the word of the writers themselves that their whole aim is to generate an atmosphere of liberality and love. If, therefore, any unlucky interruption mars the harmony of the occasion, if it is really impossible for these fraternal festivities to pass off without some silly disturbance, or somebody making a scene, it is obvious that the blame must lie with a few irritable and irritating individuals, who cannot accept these descriptions of the Trinity and the Sacrament and the Church as soothing their feelings or satisfying their ideas.

It is explained very clearly in all such statements that they are accepted by all intelligent people except those who do not accept them. But as I myself, in my political experience, have ventured to doubt the right of the Tory colonel to curse his political opponents and say it is not politics, or of the lady to love everybody and loathe Irishmen, I have the same difficulty in admitting the right of the most liberal and large-minded Christian to see good in all religions and nothing but evil in mine. But I know that to publish replies to this effect, particularly direct replies given in real controversy, will be regarded by many as a provocation and an impertinence.

Well, I must in this matter confess to being so old-fashioned as to feel something like a point of honour. I think I may say that I am normally of the sort to be sociable and get on easily with my fellows; I am not so much disposed to quarrel as to argue; and I value more than I can easily say the generally genial relations I have kept with those who differ from me merely in argument. I am very fond of England even as it is, quite apart from what it was or might be; I have a number of popular tastes, from detective stories to the defence of public-houses; I have been on many occasions on the side of the majority, as for instance in the propaganda of English patriotism during the Great War. I could even find in these sympathies a sufficient material for popular appeals; and, in a more practical sense, I should enjoy nothing more than always writing detective stories, except always reading them. But if in this much too lucky and even lazy existence I find that my co-religionists are being pelted with insults for saying that their religion is right, it would ill become me not to put myself in the way of being insulted. Many of them have had far too hard a life, and I have had far too easy a life, for me not to count it a privilege to be the object of the same curious controversial methods. If the Dean of St. Paul's really does believe, as he most undoubtedly does say, that the most devout and devoted rulers of the Catholic Church, when they accepted (realistically and even reluctantly) the fact of a modern miracle, were engaged in a "lucrative imposture, " I should very much prefer to believe that he accuses me, along with better men than myself, of becoming an impostor merely for filthy lucre. If the word "Jesuit" is still to be used as synonymous with the word "liar, " I should prefer that the same simple translation should apply to the word "Journalist, " of which it is much more often true. If the Dean accuses Catholics as Catholics of desiring innocent men to die in prison (as he does), I should much prefer that he should cast me for some part in that terrific and murderous melodrama; it might in any case be material for a detective story. In short, it is precisely because I do sympathise and agree with my Protestant and agnostic fellow countrymen, on about ninety-nine subjects out of a hundred, that I do feel it a point of honour not to avoid their accusations on these points, if they really have such accusations to bring. I am very sorry if this little book of mine seems to be controversial on subjects about which everybody is allowed to be controversial except ourselves. But I am afraid there is no help for it; and if I assure the reader that I have tried to start putting it together in an unimpaired spirit of charity, it is always possible that the charity may be as one-sided as the controversy. Anyhow, it represents my attitude towards this controversy; and it is quite possible that everything is wrong about it, except that it is right.

THE SCEPTIC AS A CRITIC

IT takes three to make a quarrel. There is needed a peacemaker. The full potentialities of human fury cannot be reached until a friend of both parties tactfully intervenes. I feel myself to be in some such position in the recent American debate about Mr. Mencken's MERCURY and the Puritans; and I admit it at the beginning with an embarrassment not untinged with terror. I know that the umpire may be torn in pieces. I know that the self-appointed umpire ought to be torn in pieces. I know, above all, that this is especially the case in anything which in any way involves international relations. Perhaps the only sound criticism is self-criticism. Perhaps this is even more true of nations than of men. And I can quite well understand that many Americans would accept suggestions from their fellow countrymen which they would rightly refuse from a foreigner. I can only plead that I have endeavoured to carry out the excellent patriotic principle of "See England First" in the equally patriotic paraphrase of "Criticize England First. " I have been engaged upon it long enough to be quite well aware that there are evils present in England that are relatively absent from America; and none more conspicuously absent, as Mr. Belloc has pointed out to the surprise of many, than the real, servile, superstitious, and mystical adoration of Money.

But what makes me so objectionable on the present occasion is that I feel a considerable sympathy with both sides. This offensive attitude I will endeavour to disguise, as far as possible, by tactfully distributed abuse of such things as I really think are abuses, and a gracefully simulated disgust with this or that part of each controversial case. But the plain truth is, that if I were an American, I should very frequently rejoice at the AMERICAN MERCURY's scoring off somebody or something; nor would my modest fireside be entirely without mild rejoicings when the AMERICAN MERCURY was scored off. But I do definitely think that both sides, and perhaps especially the iconoclastic side, need what the whole modern world needs— a fixed spiritual standard even for their own intellectual purposes. I might express it by saying that I am very fond of revolutionists, but not very fond of nihilists. For nihilists, as their name implies, have nothing to revolt about.

On this side of the matter there is little to be added to the admirably sane, subtle, and penetrating article by Mr. T. S. Eliot; * especially that vital sentence in it in which he tells Professor Irving Babbitt (who admits the need of enthusiasm) that we cannot have an enthusiasm for having an enthusiasm. I think I know, incidentally, what we must have. Professor Babbitt is a very learned man; and I myself have little Latin and less Greek. But I know enough Greek to know the meaning of the second syllable of "enthusiasm, " and I know it to be the key to this and every other discussion.

Let me take two examples, touching my points of agreement with the two sides. I heartily admire Mr. Mencken, not only for his vivacity and wit, but for his vehemence and sometimes for his violence. I warmly applaud him for his scorn and detestation of Service; and I think he was stating a historical fact when he said, as quoted in THE FORUM: "When a gang of real estate agents, bond salesmen, and automobile dealers gets together to sob for Service, it takes no Freudian to surmise that someone is about to be swindled. " I do not see why he should not call a spade a spade and a swindler a swindler. I do not blame him for using vulgar words for vulgar things. But I do remark upon two ways in which the fact of his philosophy being negative makes his criticism almost shallow. First of all, it is obvious that such a satire is entirely meaningless unless swindling is a sin. And it is equally obvious that we are instantly swallowed up in the abysses of "moralism" and "religionism, " if it is a sin. And the second point, if less obvious, is equally important— that his healthy instinct against greasy hypocrisy does not really enlighten him about the heart of that hypocrisy.

What is the matter with the cult of Service is that, like so many modern notions, it is an idolatry of the intermediate, to the oblivion of the ultimate. It is like the jargon of the idiots who talk about Efficiency without any criticism of Effect. The sin of Service is the sin of Satan: that of trying to be first where it can only be second. A word like Service has stolen the sacred capital letter from the thing which it was once supposed to serve. There is a sense in serving God, and an even more disputed sense in serving man; but there is no sense in serving Service. To serve God is at least to serve an ideal being. Even if he were an imaginary being, he would still be an ideal being. That ideal has definite and even dogmatic attributes—truth, justice, pity, purity, and the rest. To serve it, however imperfectly, is to serve a particular concept of perfection. But the man who rushes down the street waving his arms and wanting something or somebody to serve, will probably fall into the first bucket-shop or den of thieves and usurers, and be found industriously serving

The Thing

THEM. There arises the horrible idea that industry, reliability, punctuality, and business activity are good things; that mere readiness to serve the powers of this world is a Christian virtue. That is the case against Service, as distinct from the curse against Service, so heartily and inspiringly hurled by Mr. Mencken. But the serious case cannot be stated without once more raising the real question of whether mankind ought to serve anything; and of whether they had not better try to define what they intend to serve. All these silly words like Service and Efficiency and Practicality and the rest fail because they worship the means and not the end. But it all comes back to whether we do propose to worship the end; and preferably the right end.

Two other characteristic passages from Mr. Mencken will serve to show more sharply this curious sense in which he misses his own point. On the one hand, he appears to state most positively the purely personal and subjective nature of criticism; he makes it individual and almost irresponsible. "The critic is first and last simply trying to express himself; he is trying to achieve thereby for his own inner ego the grateful feeling of a function performed, a tension relieved, a katharsis attained, which Wagner achieved when he wrote DIE WALKURIE, and a hen achieves every time she lays an egg. " That is all consistent enough as far as it goes; but unfortunately Mr. Mencken appears to go on to something quite inconsistent with it. According to the quotation, he afterwards bursts into a song of triumph because there is now in America not only criticism, but controversy. "To-day for the first time in years there is strife in American criticism... ears are bitten off, noses are bloodied. There are wallops both above and below the belt. "

Now, there may be something in his case for controversy; but it is quite inconsistent with his case for creative self-expression. If the critic produces the criticism ONLY to please himself; it is entirely irrelevant that it does not please somebody else. The somebody else has a perfect right to say the exact opposite to please himself, and be perfectly satisfied with himself. But they cannot controvert because they cannot compare. They cannot compare because there is no common standard of comparison. Neither I nor anybody else can have a controversy about literature with Mr. Mencken, because there is no way of criticizing the criticism, except by asking whether the critic is satisfied. And there the debate ends, at the beginning: for nobody can doubt that Mr. Mencken is satisfied.

3

But not to make Mr. Mencken a mere victim of the ARGUMENTUM AD HOMINEM, I will make the experiment in a viler body and offer myself for dissection. I daresay a great deal of the criticism I write really is moved by a mood of self-expression; and certainly it is true enough that there is a satisfaction in self-expression. I can take something or other about which I have definite feelings—as, for instance, the philosophy of Mr. Dreiser, which has been mentioned more than once in this debate. I can achieve for my own inner ego the grateful feeling of writing as follows:

"He describes a world which appears to be a dull and discolouring illusion of indigestion, not bright enough to be called a nightmare; smelly, but not even stinking with any strength; smelling of the stale gas of ignorant chemical experiments by dirty, secretive schoolboys—the sort of boys who torture cats in corners; spineless and spiritless like a broken-backed worm; loathsomely slow and laborious like an endless slug; despairing, but not with dignity; blaspheming, but not with courage; without wit without will, without laughter or uplifting of the heart; too old to die, too deaf to leave off talking, too blind to stop, too stupid to start afresh, too dead to be killed, and incapable even of being damned, since in all its weary centuries it has not reached the age of reason. "

That is what I feel about it; and it certainly gives me pleasure to relieve my feelings. I have got it off my chest. I have attained a katharsis. I have laid an egg. I have produced a criticism, satisfying all Mr. Mencken's definitions of the critic. I have performed a function. I feel better, thank you.

But what influence my feelings can be expected to have on Mr. Dreiser, or anybody who does not admit my standards of truth and falsehood, I do not quite see. Mr. Dreiser can hardly be expected to say that his chemistry is quackery, as I think it—quackery without the liveliness we might reasonably expect from quacks. He does not think fatalism base and servile, as I do; he does not think free will the highest truth about humanity, as I do. He does not believe that despair is itself a sin, and perhaps the worst of sins, as Catholics do. He does not think blasphemy the smallest and silliest sort of pride, as even pagans do. He naturally does not think his own picture of life a false picture, resembling real life about as much as a wilderness of linoleum would resemble the land of all the living flowers, as I do. But he would not think it falser for being like a wilderness. He would probably admit that it was dreary, but think it correct to be dreary. He would probably own that he was hopeless, but not see any harm in being hopeless. What I advance as accusations, he would very probably accept as compliments.

Under these circumstances, I do not quite see how I, or anyone with my views, could have a CONTROVERSY with Mr. Dreiser. There does not seem to be any way in which I could prove him wrong, because he does not accept my view of what is wrong. There does not seem to be any way in which he could prove himself right, because I do not share his notions of what is right. We might, indeed, meet in the street and fall on each other; and while I believe we are both heavy men, I doubt not that he is the more formidable. The very possibility of our being reduced to this inarticulate explanation may possibly throw some light on Mr. Mencken's remarkable description of the new literary life in America. "Ears are bitten off, " he says; and this curious form of cultural intercourse might really be the only solution, when ears are no longer organs of hearing and there are no organs except organs of self-expression. He that hath ears to hear and will not hear may just as well have them bitten off. Such deafness seems inevitable in the creative critic, who is as indifferent as a hen to all noises except her own cackling over her own egg. Anyhow, hens do not criticize each other's eggs, or even pelt each other with eggs, in the manner of political controversy. We can only say that the novelist in question has undoubtedly laid a magnificently large and solid egg—something in the nature of an ostrich's egg; and after that, there is really nothing to prevent the ostrich from hiding its head in the sand, achieving thereby for its own inner ego the grateful feeling of a function performed. But we cannot argue with it about whether the egg is a bad egg, or whether parts of it are excellent.

In all these instances, therefore, because of the absence of a standard of ultimate values, the most ordinary functions really cannot be performed. They not only cannot be performed with "a grateful feeling, " or a katharsis, but in the long run they cannot be performed at all. We cannot really denounce the Service-mongering bond salesman as a swindler, because we have no certain agreement that it is shameful to be a swindler. A little manipulation of some of Mr. Mencken's own individualistic theories about mentality as superior to moralism might present the swindler as a superman. We cannot really argue for or against the mere ideal of Service, because neither side has really considered what is to be served or how we are to arrive at the right rules for serving it. Consequently, in practice, it may turn out that the State of Service is merely the Servile State. And finally, we cannot really argue about that or anything else, because there are no rules of the game of argument. There is nothing to prove who has scored a point and who has not. There cannot be "strife in American criticism"; the professors cannot be "forced to make some defence. " That would require plaintiffs and defendants to appear before some tribunal and give evidence according to some tests of truth. There can be a disturbance, but there can not be a discussion.

In plain words, the normal functions of man—effort, protest, judgment, persuasion, and proof—are found in fact to be hampered and hamstrung by these negations of the sceptic even when the sceptic seems at first to be only denying some distant vision or some miraculous tale. Each function is found in fact to refer to some end, to some test, to some way of distinguishing between use and misuse, which the mere sceptic destroys as completely as he could destroy any myth or superstition. If the function is only performed for the satisfaction of the performer, as in the parable of the critic and the egg, it becomes futile to discuss whether it is an addled egg. It becomes futile to consider whether eggs will produce chickens or provide breakfasts. But even to be certain of our own sanity in applying the tests, we do really have to go back to some aboriginal problem, like that of the old riddle of the priority of egg or chicken; we do really, like the great religions, have to begin AB OVO. If those primordial sanities can be disturbed, the whole of practical life can be disturbed with them. Men can be frozen by fatalism, or crazed by anarchism, or driven to death by pessimism; for men will not go on indefinitely acting on what they feel to be a fable. And it is in this organic and almost muscular sense that religion is really the help of man—in the sense that without it he is ultimately helpless, almost motionless.

Mr. Mencken and Mr. Sinclair Lewis and the other critics in the MERCURY movement are so spirited and sincere, they attack so vigorously so many things that ought to be attacked, they expose so brilliantly many things that really are impostures, that in discussing matters with them a man will have every impulse to put his cards on the table. It would be affectation and almost hypocrisy in me to ignore, in this place, the fact that I do myself believe in a special spiritual solution of this problem, a special spiritual authority above this chaos. Nor, indeed, is the idea altogether absent, as an idea, from many other minds besides my own. The Catholic philosophy is mentioned in terms of respect, and even a sort of hope, both by

Professor Babbitt** and Mr. T. S. Eliot. I do not misunderstand their courtesies, or seek to lure them a step further than they desire to go. But, as a matter of fact, by a series of faultlessly logical steps, Mr. Eliot led Professor Babbitt so near to the very gates of the Catholic Church that in the end I felt quite nervous, so to speak, for fear they should both take another unintentional step and fall into it by accident.

I have a particular reason for mentioning this matter in conclusion— a reason that is directly related to this curious effect of scepticism in weakening the normal functions of the human being. In one of the most brilliant and amusing of Mr. Sinclair Lewis's recent books there is a passage which I quote from memory, but I think more or less correctly. He said that the Catholic Faith differs from current Puritanism in that it does not ask a man to give up his sense of beauty, or his sense of humour, or his pleasant vices (by which he probably meant smoking and drinking, which are not vices at all), but that it does ask a man to give up his life and soul, his mind, body, reason, and all the rest. I ask the reader to consider, as quietly and impartially as possible, the statement thus made; and put it side by side with all those other facts about the gradual fossilizing of human function by the fundamental doubts of our day.

It would be far truer to say that the Faith gives a man back his body and his soul and his reason and his will and his very life. It would be far truer to say that the man who has received it receives all the old human functions which all the other philosophies are already taking away. It would be nearer to reality to say that he alone will have freedom, that he alone will have will, because he alone will believe in free will; that he alone will have reason, since ultimate doubt denies reason as well as authority; that he alone will truly act, because action is performed to an end. It is at least a less unlikely vision that all this hardening and hopeless despair of the intellect will leave him at last the only walking and talking citizen in a city of paralytics.

— — —

* "The Humanism of Irving Babbitt, " The Forum for July 1928.

** "The Critic and American life, " The Forum for February 1928.

IS HUMANISM A RELIGION?

I HAVE just been reading Mr. Norman Foerster's book on "American Criticism"; and I hope it is no disrespect to the bulk of the book, a series of very thoughtful studies on American thinkers, if I say that the whole point of it is in the last chapter; which propounds a certain problem or challenge to modern thought. It is the problem of whether what he calls Humanism can satisfy humanity. Of his other topics it would be easy to talk for ever. He generally says the right thing; he sometimes says the last word, in that suggestive or provocative style that tempts somebody to say one word more. In my own estimate of his subjects, Whitman would be very much larger and Lowell very much smaller. About Emerson he seems both sensitive and just; and Emerson certainly had distinction; but just that dry sort of distinction to which I should always be afraid of being unfair. A Puritan tried to be a Pagan; and succeeded in being a Pagan who hesitated about whether he ought to go and see a girl dancing. But all these things are stimulating but secondary to the question which I will take the liberty of attacking separately and attempting to answer seriously. I fear that answering it seriously must mean answering it personally. The question really is whether Humanism can perform all the functions of religion; and I cannot but regard it in relation to my own religion. It is only just to say that Humanism is quite different from Humanitarianism. It means, as explained here, something like this. Modern science and organization are in a sense only too natural. They herd us like the beasts along lines of heredity or tribal doom; they attach man to the earth like a plant instead of liberating him, even like a bird, let alone an angel. Indeed, their latest psychology is lower than the level of life. What is subconscious is sub-human and, as it were, subterranean: or something less than earthly. This fight for culture is above all a fight for consciousness: what some would call self-consciousness: but anyhow against mere subconsciousness. We need a rally of the really HUMAN things; will which is morals, memory which is tradition, culture which is the mental thrift of our fathers. Nevertheless, my first duty is to answer the question put to me; and I must answer it in the negative.

I do not believe that Humanism can be a complete substitute for Superhumanism. I do not believe it because of a certain truth to me so concrete as to be called a fact. I know it sounds very like something that has often been said in conventional or superficial apologetics. But I do not mean it in that vague sense; so far from inheriting it as a convention, I have rather recently collided with it as a discovery. I have realized it relatively late in life, and realized that it is indeed the whole story and moral of my own lifetime. But even a few years ago, when most of my moral and religious views were pretty finally formed, I should not have seen it quite sharply and clearly; as I see it now.

The fact is this: that the modern world, with its modern movements, is living on its Catholic capital. It is using, and using up, the truths that remain to it out of the old treasury of Christendom; including, of course, many truths known to pagan antiquity but crystallized in Christendom. But it is NOT really starting new enthusiasms of its own. The novelty is a matter of names and labels, like modern advertisement; in almost every other way the novelty is merely negative. It is not starting fresh things that it can really carry on far into the future. On the contrary, it is picking up old things that it cannot carry on at all. For these are the two marks of modern moral ideals. First, that they were borrowed or snatched out of ancient or mediaeval hands. Second, that they wither very quickly in modern hands. That is, very briefly, the thesis I maintain; and it so happens that the book called AMERICAN CRITICISM might almost have been meant for a text-book to prove my point.

I will begin with a particular example with which the book also deals. My whole youth was filled, as with a sunrise, with the sanguine glow of Walt Whitman. He seemed to me something like a crowd turned to a giant, or like Adam the First Man. It thrilled me to hear of somebody who had heard of somebody, who saw him in the street; it was as if Christ were still alive. I did not care about whether his unmetrical poetry were a wise form or no, any more than whether a true Gospel of Jesus were scrawled on parchment or stone. I never had a hint of the evil some enemies have attributed to him; if it was there, it was not there for me. What I saluted was a new equality, which was not a dull levelling but an enthusiastic lifting; a shouting exultation in the mere fact that men were men. Real men were greater than unreal gods; and each remained as mystic and majestic as a god, while he became as frank and comforting as a comrade. The point can be put most compactly in one of Whitman's own phrases; he says somewhere that old artists painted crowds, in which one head had a nimbus of gold-coloured light; "but I paint hundreds of heads, but paint no head without its nimbus of gold-coloured light. " A glory was to cling about men as men; a mutual worship was to take the form of fellowship; and the least and lowest of men must be included in this fellowship; a hump-backed Negro half-wit, with one eye and homicidal mania, must not be painted without his nimbus of gold-coloured light. This might seem only the final expansion of a movement begun a century before with Rousseau and the Revolutionists; and I was brought up to believe and did believe that the movement was the beginning of bigger and better things. But these were songs before sunrise; and there is no comparison between even sunrise and the sun. Whitman was brotherhood in broad daylight, showing endless varieties of radiant and wonderful creatures, all the more sacred for being solid. Shelley had adored Man, but Whitman adored Men. Every human face, every human feature, was a matter of mystical poetry, such as lit like chance torchlight, hitherto, a face here and there in the crowd. A king was a man treated as all men should be treated. A god was a man worshipped as all men should be worshipped. What could they do against a race of gods and a republic of kings; not verbally but veritably the New World?

Well... here is what Mr. Foerster says about the present position of the founder of the new world of democracy: "Our present science lends little support to an inherent 'dignity of man' or to his 'perfectibility. ' It is wholly possible that the science of the future will lead us away from democracy towards some form of aristocracy. The millennial expectations that Whitman built upon science and democracy, we are now well aware rested upon insecure foundations.... The perfection of nature, the natural goodness of man, 'the great pride of man in himself' offset with an emotional humanitarianism—these are the materials of a structure only slightly coloured with modernity. His politics, his ethics, his religion belong to the past, even that facile 'religiousness' which he hoped would suffuse and complete the work of science and democracy.... In the essentials of his prophecy, Whitman, we must conclude, has been falsified by the event. " This is a very moderate and fair statement; it would be easy to find the same thing in a much fiercer statement. Here is a monumental remark by Mr. H.L. Mencken: "They (he means certain liberal or ex-liberal thinkers) have come to realize that the morons whom they sweated to save do not want to be saved, and are not worth saving. " That is the New Spirit, if there is any New Spirit. "I will make unconquerable cities, with their arms about each other's necks, " cried Walt Whitman, "by the love of comrades, by the lifelong love of comrades. " I like to think of the face of Mr. Mencken of Baltimore, if some casual comrade from Pittsburgh tried to make him unconquerable by putting an arm around his neck. But the idea is dead for much less ferocious people than Mr. Mencken. It is dead in a man like Aldous Huxley, who complained recently of the "gratuitous" romancing of the old republican view of human nature. It is dead in the most humane and humorous of our recent critics. It is dead in so many wise and good men to-day, that I cannot help wondering whether, under modern conditions of his favourite "science, " it would not be dead in Whitman himself.

It is not dead in me. It remains real for me, not by any merit of mine, but by the fact that this mystical idea, while it has evaporated as a mood, still exists as a creed. I am perfectly prepared to assert, as firmly as I should have asserted in my boyhood, that the hump-backed and half-witted Negro is decorated with a nimbus of gold-coloured light. The truth is that Whitman's wild picture, or what he thought was a wild picture, is in fact a very old and orthodox picture. There are, as a matter of fact, any number of old pictures in which whole crowds are crowned with haloes, to indicate that they have all attained Beatitude. But for Catholics it is a fundamental dogma of the Faith that all human beings, without any exception whatever, were specially made, were shaped and pointed like shining arrows, for the end of hitting the mark of Beatitude. It is true that the shafts are feathered with free will, and therefore throw the shadow of all the tragic possibilities of free will; and that the Church (having also been aware for ages of that darker side of truth, which the new sceptics have just discovered) does also draw attention to the darkness of that potential tragedy. But that does not make any difference to the gloriousness of the potential glory. In one aspect it is even a part of it; since the freedom is itself a glory. In that sense they would still wear their haloes even in hell.

But the point is that anyone believing that all these beings were made to be blessed, and multitudes of them probably well on their way to be blessed, really has a sound philosophic reason for regarding them all as radiant and wonderful creatures, or seeing all their heads in haloes. That conviction does make every human face, every human feature, a matter of mystical poetry. But it is not at all like modern poetry. The most modern of modern poetry is not the poetry of reception, but of rejection, or rather, of repulsion. The spirit that inhabits most recent work might be called a fury of fastidiousness. The new man of letters does not get his effect by saying that for him a hump-backed Negro has a halo. He gets his effect by saying that, just as he was about to embrace finally the

11

fairest of women, he was nauseated by a pimple above her eyebrow or a stain of grease on her left thumb. Whitman tried to prove that dirty things were really clean, as when he glorified manure as the matrix of the purity of grass. His followers in free verse try to prove that clean things are really dirty; to suggest something leprous and loathsome about the thick whiteness of milk, or something prickly and plague-stricken about the unaccountable growth of hair. In short, the whole mood has changed, as a matter of poetry. But it has not changed as a matter of theology; and that is the argument for having an unchanging theology. The Catholic theology has nothing to do with democracy, for or against, in the sense of a machinery of voting or a criticism of particular political privileges. It is not committed to support what Whitman said for democracy, or even what Jefferson or Lincoln said for democracy. But it is absolutely committed to contradict what Mr. Mencken says against democracy. There will be Diocletian persecutions, there will be Dominican crusades, there will be rending of all religious peace and compromise, or even the end of civilization and the world, before the Catholic Church will admit that one single moron, or one single man, "is not worth saving."

I have therefore found in my middle age this curious fact about the lesson of my life, and that of all my generation. We all grew up with a common conviction, lit by the flames of the literary genius of Rousseau, of Shelley, of Victor Hugo, finding its final flare up and conflagration in the universalism of Walt Whitman. And we all took it for granted that all our descendants would take it for granted. I said the discovery of brotherhood seemed like the discovery of broad daylight; of something that men could never grow tired of. Yet even in my own short lifetime, men have already grown tired of it. We cannot now appeal to the love of equality as an EMOTION. We cannot now open a new book of poems, and expect it to be about the life-long love of comrades, or "Love, the beloved Republic, that feeds upon freedom and lives." We realize that in most men it has died, because it was a mood and not a doctrine. And we begin to wonder too late, in the wise fashion of the aged, how we could ever have expected it to last as a mood, if it was not strong enough to last as a doctrine. And we also begin to realize that all the real strength there was in it, which is the only strength that remains in it, was the original strength of the doctrine. What really happened was this: that the men of the eighteenth century, many of them in a just impatience with corrupt and cynical priests, turned on those priests and said in effect, "Well, I suppose you call yourselves Christians; so you can't actually DENY that men are brothers or that it is our duty to help the poor. " The very confidence of their challenge, the very ringing note in the revolutionary voice, came from the fact that the Christian reactionaries were in a false position as Christians. The democratic demand won because it seemed unanswerable. And it seemed unanswerable, not in the least because it is unanswerable, but because even decadent Christians dared not give the answer. Mr. H. L. Mencken will always be happy to oblige with the answer.

Now, it was just here that, for me, the business began to be odd and interesting. For, looking back on older religious crises, I seem to see a certain coincidence, or rather, a set of things too coincident to be called a coincidence After all, when I come to think of it, all the other revolts against the Church, before the Revolution and especially since the Reformation, had told the same strange story. Every great heretic had always exhibit three remarkable characteristics in combination. First, he picked out some mystical idea from the Church's bundle or balance of mystical ideas. Second, he used that one mystical idea against all the other mystical ideas. Third (and most singular), he seems generally to have had no notion that his own favourite mystical idea was a mystical idea, at least in the sense of a mysterious or dubious or dogmatic idea. With a queer uncanny innocence, he seems always to have taken this one thing for granted. He assumed it to be unassailable, even when he was using it to assail all sorts of similar things. The most popular and obvious example is the Bible. To an impartial pagan or sceptical observer, it must always seem the strangest story in the world; that men rushing in to wreck a temple, overturning the altar and driving out the priest, found there certain sacred volumes inscribed "Psalms" or "Gospels"; and (instead of throwing them on the fire with the rest) began to use them as infallible oracles rebuking all the other arrangements. If the sacred high altar was all wrong, why were the secondary sacred documents necessarily all right? If the priest had faked his Sacraments, why could he not have faked his Scriptures? Yet it was long before it even occurred to those who brandished this one piece of Church furniture to break up all the other Church furniture that anybody could be so profane as to examine this one fragment of furniture itself. People were quite surprised, and in some parts of the world are still surprised, that anybody should dare to do so.

Again, the Calvinists took the Catholic idea of the absolute knowledge and power of God; and treated it as a rocky irreducible truism so solid that anything could be built on it, however crushing or cruel. They were so confident in their logic, and its one first principle of predestination, that they tortured the intellect and imagination with dreadful deductions about God, that seemed to turn Him into a demon. But it never seems to have struck them that somebody might suddenly say that he did not believe in the demon. They were quite surprised when people called "infidels" here and there began to say it. They had assumed the Divine foreknowledge as so fixed, that it must, if necessary, fulfil itself by destroying the Divine mercy. They never thought anybody would deny the knowledge exactly as they denied the mercy. Then came Wesley and the reaction against Calvinism; and Evangelicals seized on the very Catholic idea that mankind has a sense of sin; and they wandered about offering everybody release from his mysterious burden of sin. It is a proverb, and almost a joke, that they address a stranger in the street and offer to relax his secret agony of sin. But it seldom seemed to strike them, until much later, that the man in the street might possibly answer that he did not want to be saved from sin, any more than from spotted fever or St. Vitus's Dance; because these things were not in fact causing him any suffering at all. They, in their turn, were quite surprised when the result of Rousseau and the revolutionary optimism began to express itself in men claiming a purely human happiness and dignity; a contentment with the comradeship of their kind; ending with the happy yawp of Whitman that he would not "lie awake and weep for his sins. "

Now the plain truth is that Shelley and Whitman and the revolutionary optimists were themselves doing exactly the same thing all over again. They also, though less consciously because of the chaos of their times, had really taken out of the old Catholic tradition one particular transcendental idea; the idea that there is a spiritual dignity in man as man, and a universal duty to love men as men. And they acted in exactly the same extraordinary fashion as their prototypes, the Wesleyans and the Calvinists. They took it for granted that this spiritual idea was absolutely self-evident like the sun and moon; that nobody could ever destroy that, though in the name of it they destroyed everything else. They perpetually hammered away at their human divinity and human dignity, and inevitable love for all human beings; as if these things were naked natural facts. And now they are quite surprised when new and restless realists suddenly explode, and begin to say that a pork-butcher with red whiskers and a wart on his nose does not strike them as particularly divine or dignified, that they are not conscious of the smallest sincere impulse to love him, that they could not love him if they tried, or that they do not recognize any particular obligation to try.

It might appear that the process has come to an end, and that there is nothing more for the naked realist to shed. But it is not so; and the process can still go on. There are still traditional charities to which men cling. There are still traditional charities for them to fling away when they find they are only traditional. Everybody must have noticed in the most modern writers the survival of a rather painful sort of pity. They no longer honour all men, like St. Paul and the other mystical democrats. It would hardly be too much to say that they despise all men; often (to do them justice) including themselves. But they do in a manner pity all men, and particularly those that are pitiable; by this time they extend the feeling almost disproportionately to the other animals. This compassion for men is also tainted with its historical connection with Christian charity; and even in the case of animals, with the example of many Christian saints. There is nothing to show that a new revulsion from such sentimental religions will not free men even from the obligation of pitying the pain of the world. Not only Nietzsche, but many Neo-Pagans working on his lines, have suggested such hardness as a higher intellectual purity. And having read many modern poems about the Man of the Future, made of steel and illumined with nothing warmer than green fire, I have no difficulty in imagining a literature that should pride itself on a merciless and metallic detachment. Then, perhaps, it might be faintly conjectured that the last of the Christian virtues had died. But so long as they lived they were Christian.

I do not therefore believe that Humanism and Religion are rivals on equal terms. I believe it is a rivalry between the pools and the fountain; or between the firebrands and the fire. Each of these old intellectuals snatched one firebrand out of the undying fire; but the point is that though he waved the torch very wildly, though he would have used the torch to burn down half the world, the torch went out very soon. The Puritans did not really perpetuate their sublime exultation in helplessness; they only made it unpopular. We did not go on indefinitely looking at the Brooklyn crowds with the eye of Whitman; we have come with singular rapidity to regard them with the eye of Dreiser. In short, I distrust spiritual experiments outside the central spiritual tradition; for the simple reason that I think they do not last, even if they manage to spread. At the most they stand for one generation; at the commonest for one fashion; at the lowest for one clique. I do not think they have the secret of continuity; certainly not of corporate continuity. For an antiquated, doddering old democrat like myself may be excused for attaching some slight importance to that last question; that of covering the common life of mankind. How many Humanists are there supposed to be among the inferior crowd of human beings? Are there to be, for instance, no more than there were Greek philosophers in an ordinary rabble of jolly pagan polytheistic Greeks? Are there to be no more than there were men concentrated on the Culture of Matthew Arnold, among the mobs who followed Cardinal Manning or General Booth? I do not in the least intend to sneer at Humanism; I think I understand the intellectual distinction it draws, and I have tried to understand it in a spirit of humility; but I feel a faint interest in how many people out of the battered and bewildered human race are actually expected to understand it. And I ask with a certain personal interest; for there are three hundred million people in the world who accept the mysteries that I accept and live by the faith I hold. I really want to know whether it is anticipated that there will be three hundred million Humanists in Humanity. The sanguine may say that Humanism will be the religion of the next generation, just as Comte said that Humanity would be the God of the next generation; and so in one sense it was. But it is not the God of this generation. And the question is what will be the religion of the next generation after that, or all the other generations (as a certain ancient promise ran) even unto the end of the world.

Humanism, in Mr. Foerster's sense, has one very wise and worthy character. It is really trying to pick up the pieces; that is, to pick up all the pieces. All that was done before was first blind destruction and then random and scrappy selection; as if boys had broken up a stained-glass window and then made a few scraps into coloured spectacles, the rose-coloured spectacles of the republican or the green or yellow spectacles of the pessimist and the decadent. But Humanism as here professed will stoop to gather all it can; for instance, it is great enough to stoop and pick up the jewel of humility. Mr. Foerster does understand, as the eighteenth and nineteenth centuries did not understand, the case for humility. Matthew Arnold, who made something of the same stand for what he called Culture in the mid-nineteenth century, attempted something of the same preservation of chastity; which he would call, in a rather irritating manner, "pureness. " But before we call either Culture or Humanism a substitute for religion, there is a very plain question that can be asked in the form of a very homely metaphor. Humanism may try to pick up the pieces; but can it stick them together? Where is the cement which made religion corporate and popular, which can prevent it falling to pieces in a debris of individualistic tastes and degrees? What is to prevent one Humanist wanting chastity without humility, and another humility without chastity, and another truth or beauty without either? The problem of an enduring ethic and culture consists in finding an arrangement of the pieces by which they remain related, as do the stones arranged in an arch. And I know only one scheme that has thus proved its solidity, bestriding lands and ages with its gigantic arches, and carrying everywhere the high river of baptism upon an aqueduct of Rome.

THE DRIFT FROM DOMESTICITY

IN the matter of reforming things, as distinct from deforming them, there is one plain and simple principle; a principle which will probably be called a paradox. There exists in such a case a certain institution or law; let us say for the sake of simplicity, a fence or gate erected across a road. The more modern type of reformer goes gaily up to it and says, "I don't see the use of this; let us clear it away. " To which the more intelligent type of reformer will do well to answer: "If you don't see the use of it, I certainly won't let you clear it away. Go away and think. Then, when you can come back and tell me that you do see the use of it, I may allow you to destroy it. "

This paradox rests on the most elementary common sense. The gate or fence did not grow there. It was not set up by somnambulists who built it in their sleep. It is highly improbable that it was put there by escaped lunatics who were for some reason loose in the street. Some person had some reason for thinking it would be a good thing for somebody. And until we know what the reason was, we really cannot judge whether the reason was reasonable. It is extremely probable that we have overlooked some whole aspect of the question, if something set up by human beings like ourselves seems to be entirely meaningless and mysterious. There are reformers who get over this difficulty by assuming that all their fathers were fools; but if that be so, we can only say that folly appears to be a hereditary disease. But the truth is that nobody has any business to destroy a social institution until he has really seen it as an historical institution. If he knows how it arose, and what purposes it was supposed to serve, he may really be able to say that they were bad purposes, or that they have since become bad purposes, or that they are purposes which are no longer served. But if he simply stares at the thing as a senseless monstrosity that has somehow sprung up in his path, it is he and not the traditionalist who is suffering from an illusion. We might even say that he is seeing things in a nightmare. This principle applies to a thousand things, to trifles as well as true institutions, to convention as well as to conviction. It was exactly the sort of person, like Joan of Arc, who did know why women wore skirts, who was most justified in not wearing one; it was exactly the sort of person, like St. Francis, who did sympathise with the feast and the fireside, who was most entitled to become a beggar on the open road. And when, in the general emancipation of modern society, the Duchess says she does not see why she shouldn't play leapfrog, or the Dean declares that he sees no valid canonical reason why he should not stand on his head, we may say to these persons with patient benevolence: "Defer, therefore, the operation you contemplate until you have realised by ripe reflection what principle or prejudice you are violating. Then play leapfrog and stand on your head and the Lord be with you. "

Among the traditions that are being thus attacked, not intelligently but most unintelligently, is the fundamental human creation called the Household or the Home. That is a typical thing which men attack, not because they can see through it, but because they cannot see it at all. They beat at it blindly, in a fashion entirely haphazard and opportunist; and many of them would pull it down without even pausing to ask why it was ever put up. It is true that only a few of them would have avowed this object in so many words. That only proves how very blind and blundering they are. But they have fallen into a habit of mere drift and gradual detachment from family life; something that is often merely accidental and devoid of any definite theory at all. But though it is accidental it is none the less anarchical. And it is all the more anarchical for not being anarchist. It seems to be largely founded on individual irritation; an irritation which varies with the individual. We are merely told that in this or that case a particular temperament was tormented by a particular environment; but nobody even explained how the evil arose, let alone whether the evil is really escaped. We are told that in this or that family Grandmamma talked a great deal of nonsense, which God knows is true; or that it is very difficult to have intimate intellectual relations with Uncle Gregory without telling him he is a fool, which is indeed the case. But nobody seriously considers the remedy, or even the malady; or whether the existing individualistic dissolution is a remedy at all. Much of this business began with the influence of Ibsen, a very powerful dramatist and an exceedingly feeble philosopher. I suppose that Nora of THE DOLL'S HOUSE was intended to be an inconsequent person; but certainly her most inconsequent action was her last. She complained that she was not yet fit to look after children, and then proceeded to get as far as possible from the children, that she might study them more closely.

There is one simple test and type of this neglect of scientific thinking and the sense of a social rule; the neglect which has now left us with nothing but a welter of exceptions. I have read hundreds and thousands of times, in all the novels and newspapers of our epoch, certain phrases about the just right of the young to liberty, about the unjust claim of the elders to control, about the conception that all souls must be free or all citizens equal, about the absurdity of authority or the degradation of obedience. I am not arguing those matters directly at the moment. But what strikes me as astounding, in a logical sense, is that not one of these myriad novelists and newspaper-men ever seems to think of asking the next and most obvious question. It never seems to occur to them to enquire what becomes of the opposite obligation. If the child is free from the first to disregard the parent, why is not the parent free from the first to disregard the child? If Mr. Jones, Senior, and Mr. Jones, Junior, are only two free and equal citizens, why should one citizen sponge on another citizen for the first fifteen years of his life? Why should the elder Mr. Jones be expected to feed, clothe and shelter out of his own pocket another person who is entirely free of any obligations to him? If the bright young thing cannot be asked to tolerate her grandmother, who has become something of a bore, why should the grandmother or the mother have tolerated the bright young thing at a period of her life when she was by no means bright? Why did they laboriously look after her at a time when her contributions to the conversation were seldom epigrammatic and not often intelligible? Why should Jones Senior stand drinks and free meals to anybody so unpleasant as Jones Junior, especially in the immature phases of his existence? Why should he not throw the baby out of the window; or at any rate, kick the boy out of doors? It is obvious that we are dealing with a real relation, which may be equality, but is certainly not similarity.

Some social reformers try to evade this difficulty, I know, by some vague notions about the State or an abstraction called Education eliminating the parental function. But this, like many notions of solid scientific persons, is a wild illusion of the nature of mere moonshine. It is based on that strange new superstition, the idea of infinite resources of organisation. It is as if officials grew like grass or bred like rabbits. There is supposed to be an endless supply of salaried persons, and of salaries for them; and they are to undertake all that human beings naturally do for themselves; including the care of children. But men cannot live by taking in each other's baby-linen. They cannot provide a tutor for each citizen; who is to tutor the tutors? Men cannot be educated by machinery; and though there might be a Robot bricklayer or scavenger, there will never be a Robot schoolmaster or governess. The actual effect of this theory is that one harassed person has to look after a hundred children, instead of one normal person looking after a normal number of them. Normally that normal person is urged by a natural force, which costs nothing and does not require a salary; the force of natural affection for his young, which exists even among the animals. If you cut off that natural force, and substitute a paid bureaucracy, you are like a fool who should pay men to turn the wheel of his mill, because he refused to use wind or water which he could get for nothing. You are like a lunatic who should carefully water his garden with a watering-can, while holding up an umbrella to keep off the rain.

It is now necessary to recite these truisms; for only by doing so can we begin to get a glimpse of that REASON for the existence of the family, which I began this essay by demanding. They were all familiar to our fathers, who believed in the links of kinship and also in the links of logic. To-day our logic consists mostly of missing links; and our family largely of absent members. But, anyhow, this is the right end at which to begin any such enquiry; and not at the tail-end or the fag-end of some private muddle, by which Dick has become discontented or Susan has gone off on her own. If Dick or Susan wish to destroy the family because they do not see the use of it, I say as I said in the beginning; if they do not see the use of it, they had much better preserve it. They have no business even to think of destroying it until they have seen the use of it.

But it has other uses, besides the obvious fact that it means a necessary social work being done for love when it cannot be done for money; and (one might almost dare to hint) presumably to be repaid with love since it is never repaid in money. On that simple side of the matter the general situation is easy to record. The existing and general system of society, subject in our own age and industrial culture to very gross abuses and painful problems, is nevertheless a normal one. It is the idea that the commonwealth is made up of a number of small kingdoms, of which a man and a woman become the king and queen and in which they exercise a reasonable authority, subject to the common sense of the commonwealth, until those under their care grow up to found similar kingdoms and exercise similar authority. This is the social structure of mankind, far older than all its records and more universal than any of its religions; and all attempts to alter it are mere talk and tomfoolery.

But the other advantage of the small group is now not so much neglected as simply not realised. Here again we have some extraordinary delusions spread all over the literature and journalism of our time. Those delusions now exist in such a degree that we may say, for all practical purposes, that when a thing has been stated about a thousand times as obviously true, it is almost certain to be obviously false. One such statement may be specially noted here. There is undoubtedly something to be said against domesticity and in favour of the general drift towards life in hotels, clubs, colleges, communal settlements and the rest; or for a social life organised on the plan of the great commercial systems of our time. But the truly extraordinary suggestion is often made that this escape from the home is an escape into greater freedom. The change is actually offered as favourable to liberty.

To anybody who can think, of course, it is exactly the opposite. The domestic division of human society is not perfect, being human. It does not achieve complete liberty; a thing somewhat difficult to do or even to define. But it is a mere matter of arithmetic that it puts a larger number of people in supreme control of something, and able to shape it to their personal liking, than do the vast organisations that rule society outside; whether those systems are legal or commercial or even merely social. Even if we were only considering the parents, it is plain that there are more parents than there are policemen or politicians or heads of big businesses or proprietors of hotels. As I shall suggest in a moment, the argument actually applies indirectly to the children as well as directly to the parents. But the main point is that the world OUTSIDE the home is now under a rigid discipline and routine and it is only inside the home that there is really a place for individuality and liberty. Anyone stepping out of the front-door is obliged to step into a procession, all going the same way and to a great extent even obliged to wear the same uniform. Business, especially big business, is now organised like an army. It is, as some would say, a sort of mild militarism without bloodshed; as I should say, a militarism without the military virtues. But anyhow, it is obvious that a hundred clerks in a bank or a hundred waitresses in a teashop are more regimented and under rule than the same individuals when each has gone back to his or her own dwelling or lodging, hung with his or her favourite pictures or fragrant with his or her favourite cheap cigarettes. But this, which is so obvious in the commercial case, is no less true even in the social case. In practice, the pursuit of pleasure is merely the pursuit of fashion. The pursuit of fashion is merely the pursuit of convention; only that it happens to be a new convention. The jazz dances, the joy rides, the big pleasure parties and hotel entertainments, do not make any more provision for a REALLY independent taste than did any of the fashions of the past. If a wealthy young lady wants to do what all the other wealthy young ladies are doing, she will find it great fun, simply because youth is fun and society is fun. She will enjoy being modern exactly as her Victorian grandmother enjoyed being Victorian. And quite right too; but it is the enjoyment of convention, not the enjoyment of liberty. It is perfectly healthy for all young people of all historic periods to herd together, to a reasonable extent, and enthusiastically copy each other. But in that there is nothing particularly fresh and certainly nothing particularly free. The girl who likes shaving her head and powdering her nose and wearing short skirts will find the world organised for her and will march happily with the procession. But a girl who happened to like having her hair down to her heels or loading herself with barbaric gauds and trailing garments or (most awful of all) leaving her nose in its natural state— she will still be well advised to do these things on her own premises. If the Duchess does want to play leap frog, she must not start suddenly leaping in the manner of a frog across the ballroom of the Babylon Hotel, when it is crowded with the fifty best couples professionally practising the very latest dance, for the instruction of society. The Duchess will find it easier to practise leap frog to the admiration of her intimate friends in the old oak-panelled hall of Fitzdragon Castle. If the Dean must stand on his head, he will do it with more ease and grace in the calm atmosphere of the Deanery than by attempting to interrupt the programme of some social entertainment already organised for philanthropic purposes.

If there is this impersonal routine in commercial and even in social things, it goes without saying that it exists and always must exist in political and legal things. For instance, the punishments of the State must be sweeping generalisations. It is only the punishments of the home that can possibly be adapted to the individual case; because it is only there that the judge can know anything of the individual. If Tommy takes a silver thimble out of a work-basket, his mother may act very differently according as she knows that he did it for fun or for spite or to sell to somebody, or to get somebody into trouble. But if Tomkins takes a silver thimble out of a shop, the law not only can but must punish him according to the rule made for all shoplifters or stealers of silver. It is only the domestic discipline that can show any sympathy or especially any humour. I do not say that the family always does do this; but I say that the State never ought to attempt it. So that even if we consider the parents alone as independent princes, and the children merely as subjects, the relative freedom of the family can and often does work to the advantage of those subjects. But so long as the children are children, they will always be the subjects of somebody. The question is whether they are to be distributed naturally under their natural princes, as the old phrase went, who normally feel for them what nobody else will feel, a natural affection. It seems to me clear that this normal distribution gives the largest amount of liberty to the largest number of people.

My complaint of the anti-domestic drift is that it is unintelligent. People do not know what they are doing; because they do not know what they are undoing. There are a multitude of modern manifestations, from the largest to the smallest, ranging from a divorce to a picnic party. But each is a separate escape or evasion; and especially an evasion of the point at issue. People ought to decide in a philosophical fashion whether they desire the traditional social order or not; or if there is any particular alternative to be desired. As it is they treat the public question merely as a mess or medley of private questions. Even in being anti-domestic they are much too domestic in their test of domesticity. Each family considers only its own case and the result is merely narrow and negative. Each case is an exception to a rule that does not exist. The family, especially in the modern state, stands in need of considerable correction and reconstruction; most things do in the modern state. But the family mansion should be preserved or destroyed or rebuilt; it should not be allowed to fall to pieces brick by brick because nobody has any historic sense of the object of bricklaying. For instance, the architects of the restoration should rebuild the house with wide and easily opened doors, for the practice of the ancient virtue of hospitality. In other words, private property should be distributed with sufficiently decent equality to allow of a margin for festive intercourse. But the hospitality of a house will always be different from the hospitality of a hotel. And it will be different in being more individual, more independent, more interesting than the hospitality of a hotel. It is perfectly right that the young Browns and the young Robinsons should meet and mix and dance and make asses of themselves, according to the design of their Creator. But there will always be some difference between the Browns entertaining the Robinsons and the Robinsons entertaining the Browns. And it will be a difference to the advantage of variety, of personality, of the potentialities of the mind of man; or, in other words, of life, liberty and the pursuit of happiness.

LOGIC AND LAWN TENNIS

WHEN we say that we doubt the intellectual improvement produced by Protestantism and Rationalism and the modern world, there generally arises a very confused controversy, which is a sort of tangle of terminology. But, broadly speaking, the difference between us and our critics is this. They mean by growth an increase of the tangle; whereas we mean by thought a disentangling of the tangle. Even a short and simple length of straight and untangled wire is worth more to us than whole forests of mere entanglement. That there are more topics talked about, or more terms used, or more people using them, or more books and other authorities cited— all this is nothing to us if people misuse the terms, misunderstand the topics, invoke the authorities at random and without the use of reason; and finally bring out a false result. A peasant who merely says, "I have five pigs; if I kill one I shall have four pigs, " is thinking in an extremely simple and elementary way; but he is thinking as clearly and correctly as Aristotle or Euclid. But suppose he reads or half-reads newspapers and books of popular science. Suppose he starts to call one pig the Land and another pig Capital and a third pig Exports, and finally brings out the result that the more pigs he kills the more he possesses; or that every sow that litters decreases the number of pigs in the world. He has learnt economic terminology, merely as a means of becoming entangled in economic fallacy. It is a fallacy he could never have fallen into while he was grounded in the divine dogma that Pigs is Pigs. Now for that sort of intellectual instruction and advancement we have no use at all; and in that sense only it is true that we prefer the ignorant peasant to the instructed pedant. But that is not because we think ignorance better than instruction or barbarism better than culture. It is merely that we think a short length of the untangled logical chain is better than an interminable length of it that is interminably tangled. It is merely that we prefer a man to do a sum of simple addition right than a sum in long division wrong.

Now what we observe about the whole current culture of journalism and general discussion is that people do not know how to begin to think. Not only is their thinking at third and fourth hand, but it always starts about three-quarters of the way through the process. Men do not know where their own thoughts came from. They do not know what their own words imply. They come in at the end of every controversy and know nothing of where it began or what it is all about. They are constantly assuming certain absolutes, which, if correctly defined, would strike even themselves as being not absolutes but absurdities. To think thus is to be in a tangle; to go on thinking is to be in more and more of a tangle. And at the back of all there is always something understood; which is really something misunderstood.

For instance, I read an article by the admirable Mr. Tilden, the great tennis-player, who was debating what is wrong with English Tennis. "Nothing can save English Tennis, " he said, except certain reforms of a fundamental sort, which he proceeded to explain. The English, it appears, have a weird and unnatural way of regarding tennis as a game, or thing to be enjoyed. He admitted that this has been part of a sort of amateur spirit in everything which is (as he very truly noted) also a part of the national character. But all this stands in the way of what he called saving English Tennis. He meant what some would call making it perfect, and others would call making it professional. Now, I take that as a very typical passage, taken from the papers at random, and containing the views of a keen and acute person on a subject that he thoroughly understands. But what he does not understand is the thing which he supposes to be understood. He thoroughly knows his subject and yet he does not know what he is talking about; because he does not know what he is taking for granted. He does not realise the relation of means and ends, or axioms and inferences, in his own philosophy. And nobody would probably be more surprised and even legitimately indignant than he, if I were to say that the first principles of his philosophy appear to be as follows: (1) There is in the nature of things a certain absolute and divine Being, whose name is Mr. Lawn Tennis. (2) All men exist for the good and glory of this Mr. Tennis and are bound to approximate to his perfections and fulfil his will. (3) To this higher duty they are bound to surrender their natural desire for enjoyment in this life. (4) They are bound to put this loyalty first; and to love it more passionately than patriotic tradition, the preservation of their own national type and national culture; not to mention even their national virtues. That is the creed or scheme of doctrine that is here developed without being defined. The only way for us to save the game of Lawn Tennis is to prevent it from being a game. The only way to save English Tennis is to prevent it from being English. It does not occur to such thinkers that some people may possibly like it because it is English and enjoy it because it is enjoyable. There is some abstract divine standard in the thing, to which it is everybody's duty to rise, at any sacrifice of pleasure or affection. When Christians say this of the sacrifices made for Christ, it sounds rather a hard saying. But when tennis-players say it about the sacrifices demanded by tennis, it sounds quite ordinary and casual in the confusion of current thought and expression. And nobody notices that a sort of human sacrifice is being offered to a sort of new and nameless god.

In the good old days of Victorian rationalism it used to be the conventional habit to scoff at St. Thomas Aquinas and the mediaeval theologians; and especially to repeat perpetually a well-worn joke about the man who discussed how many angels could dance on the point of a needle. The comfortable and commercial Victorians, with their money and merchandise, might well have felt a sharper end of the same needle, even if it was the other end of it. It would have been good for their souls to have looked for that needle, not in the haystack of mediaeval metaphysics, but in the neat needle-case of their own favourite pocket Bible. It would have been better for them to meditate, not on how many angels could go on the point of a needle, but on how many camels could go through the eye of it. But there is another comment on this curious joke or catchword, which is more relevant to our purpose here. If the mediaeval mystic ever did argue about angels standing on a needle, at least he did not argue as if the object of angels was to stand on a needle; as if God had created all the Angels and Archangels, all the Thrones, Virtues, Powers and Principalities, solely in order that there might be something to clothe and decorate the unseemly nakedness of the point of a needle. But that is the way that modern rationalists reason. The mediaeval mystic would not even have said that a needle exists to be a standing-ground for angels. The mediaeval mystic would have been the first to say that a needle exists to make clothes for men. For mediaeval mystics, in their dim transcendental way, were much interested in the real reasons for things and the distinction between the means and the end. They wanted to know what a thing was really for, and what was the dependence of one idea on another. And they might even have suggested, what so many journalists seem to forget, the paradoxical possibility that Tennis was made for Man and not Man for Tennis.

The Modernists were peculiarly unfortunate when they said that the modern world must not be expected to tolerate the old syllogistic methods of the Schoolmen. They were proposing to scrap the one mediaeval instrument which the modern world will most immediately require. There would have been a far better case for saying that the revival of Gothic architecture has been sentimental and futile; that the Pre-Raphaelite movement in art was only an eccentric episode; that the fashionable use of the word "Guild" for every possible sort of social institution was affected and artificial; that the feudalism of Young England was very different from that of Old England. But this method of clean-cut deduction, with the definition of the postulates and the actual answering of the question, is something of which the whole of our newspaper-flattered society is in sharp and instant need; as the poisoned are in need of medicine. I have here taken only one example which happened to catch my eye out of a hundred thousand that flash past every hour. And as Tennis, like every other good game, has to be played with the head as well as the hand, I think it highly desirable that it should be occasionally discussed at least as intelligently as it is played.

OBSTINATE ORTHODOXY

I HAVE been asked to explain something about myself which seems to be regarded as very extraordinary. The problem has been presented to me in the form of a cutting from a very flattering American article, which yet contained a certain suggestion of wonder. So far as I can understand, it is thought extraordinary that a man should be ordinary. I am ordinary in the correct sense of the term; which means the acceptance of an order; a Creator and the Creation, the common sense of gratitude for Creation, life and love as gifts permanently good, marriage and chivalry as laws rightly controlling them, and the rest of the normal traditions of our race and religion. It is also thought a little odd that I regard the grass as green, even after some newly-discovered Slovak artist has painted it grey; that I think daylight very tolerable in spite of thirteen Lithuanian philosophers sitting in a row and cursing the light of day; and that, in matters more polemical, I actually prefer weddings to divorces and babies to Birth Control. These eccentric views, which I share with the overwhelming majority of mankind, past and present, I should not attempt to defend here one by one. And I only give a general reply for a particular reason. I wish to make it unmistakably plain that my defence of these sentiments is not sentimental. It would be easy to gush about these things; but I defy the reader, after reading this, to find the faintest trace of the tear of sensibility. I hold this view not because it is sensibility, but because it is sense.

On the contrary, it is the sceptics who are the sentimentalists. More than half the "revolt" and the talk of being advanced and progressive is simply a weak sort of snobbishness which takes the form of a worship of Youth. Some men of my generation delight in declaring that they are of the Party of the Young and defending every detail of the latest fashions or freaks. If I do not do that, it is for the same reason that I do not dye my hair or wear stays. But even when it is less despicable than that, the current phrase that everything must be done for youth, that the rising generation is all that matters, is in sober fact a piece of pure sentimentalism. It is also, within reason, a perfectly natural piece of sentiment. All healthy people like to see the young enjoying themselves; but if we turn that pleasure into a principle, we are sentimentalists. If we desire the greatest happiness of the greatest number, it will be obvious that the greatest number, at any given moment, are rather more likely to be between twenty-five and seventy than to be between seventeen and twenty-five. Sacrificing everything to the young will be like working only for the rich. They will be a privileged class and the rest will be snobs or slaves. Moreover, the young will always have a fair amount of fun under the worst conditions; if we really wish to console the world, it will be much more rational to console the old. This is what I call facing facts; and I have continued to believe in most of these traditions because they are facts. I could give a great many other examples; for instance, chivalry. Chivalry is not the romantic, but the realistic, view of the sexes. It is so realistic that the real reasons for it cannot always be given in print.

If those called free-thinkers are sentimentalists, those called free-lovers are open and obvious sentimentalists. We can always convict such people of sentimentalism by their weakness for euphemism. The phrase they use is always softened and suited for journalistic appeals. They talk of free love when they mean something quite different, better defined as free lust. But being sentimentalists they feel bound to simper and coo over the word "love. " They insist on talking about Birth Control when they mean less birth and no control. We could smash them to atoms, if we could be as indecent in our language as they are immoral in their conclusions. And as it is with morals, so it is with religion. The general notion that science establishes agnosticism is a sort of mystification produced by talking Latin and Greek instead of plain English. Science is the Latin for knowledge. Agnosticism is the Greek for ignorance. It is not self-evident that ignorance is the goal of knowledge. It is the ignorance and not the knowledge that produces the current notion that free thought weakens theism. It is the real world, that we see with our own eyes, that obviously unfolds a plan of things that fit into each other. It is only a remote and misty legend that ever pretended to explain it by the automatic advantage of the "fit. " As a fact, modern evolutionists, even when they are still Darwinians, do not pretend that the theory explains all varieties and adaptations. Those who know are rather rescuing Darwin at the expense of Darwinism. But it is those who do not know who doubt or deny; it is typical that their myth is actually called the Missing Link. They actually know nothing of their own argument except that it breaks down somewhere. But it is worth while to ask why this loose legend has such power over many; and I will proceed to my suggestion. I have not changed my mind; nor, indeed, have they changed their mind. They have only changed their mood.

What we call the intellectual world is divided into two types of people—those who worship the intellect and those who use it. There are exceptions; but, broadly speaking, they are never the same people. Those who use the intellect never worship it; they know too much about it. Those who worship the intellect never use it; as you can see by the things they say about it. Hence there has arisen a confusion about intellect and intellectualism; and, as the supreme expression of that confusion, something that is called in many countries the Intelligentsia, and in France more especially, the Intellectuals. It is found in practice to consist of clubs and coteries of people talking mostly about books and pictures, but especially new books and new pictures; and about music, so long as it is very modern music; or what some would call very unmusical music. The first fact to record about it is that what Carlyle said of the world is very specially true of the intellectual world— that it is mostly fools. Indeed, it has a curious attraction for complete fools, as a warm fire has for cats. I have frequently visited such societies, in the capacity of a common or normal fool, and I have almost always found there a few fools who were more foolish than I had imagined to be possible to man born of woman; people who had hardly enough brains to be called half-witted. But it gave them a glow within to be in what they imagined to be the atmosphere of intellect; for they worshipped it like an unknown god. I could tell many stories of that world. I remember a venerable man with a very long beard who seemed to live at one of these clubs. At intervals he would hold up his hand as if for silence and preface his remarks by saying, "A Thought. " And then he would say something that sounded as if a cow had suddenly spoken in a drawing-room. I remember once a silent and much-enduring man (I rather think it was my friend Mr. Edgar Jepson, the novelist) who could bear it no longer and cried with a sort of expiring gasp, "But, Good God, man, you don't call that a THOUGHT, do you? " But that was pretty much the quality of the thought of such thinkers, especially of the freethinkers. Out of this social situation arises one sort of exception to the rule. Intelligence does exist even in the Intelligentsia. It does sometimes happen that a man of real talent has a weakness for flattery, even the flattery of fools. He would rather say something that silly people think clever than something which only clever people could perceive to be true. Oscar Wilde was a man of this type. When he said somewhere that an immoral woman is the sort of woman a man never gets tired of, he used a phrase so baseless as to be perfectly pointless. Everybody knows that a man may get tired of a whole procession of immoral women, especially if he is an immoral man. That was "a Thought";

otherwise something to be uttered, with uplifted hand, to people who could not think at all. In their poor muddled minds there was some vague connection between wit and cynicism; so they never applauded him so warmly as a wit, as when he was cynical without being witty. But when he said, "A cynic is a man who knows the price of everything and the value of nothing, " he made a statement (in excellent epigrammatic form) which really meant something. But it would have meant his own immediate dethronement if it could have been understood by those who only enthroned him for being cynical.

Anyhow, it is in this intellectual world, with its many fools and few wits and fewer wise men, that there goes on perpetually a sort of ferment of fashionable revolt and negation. From this comes all that is called destructive criticism; though, as a matter of fact, the new critic is generally destroyed by the next critic long before he has had any chance of destroying anything else. When people say solemnly that the world is in revolt against religion or private property or patriotism or marriage, they mean that this world is in revolt against them; or rather, is in permanent revolt against everything. Now, as a matter of fact, this world has a certain excuse for being always in that state of excitement, apart from mere fuss and mere folly. The reason is rather an important one; and I would ask anyone who really does want to think, and especially to think freely, to pause upon it seriously for a moment. It arises from the fact that these people are so much concerned with the study of Art. It collapses into mere drivelling and despair, because they try to transfer their treatment of art to the treatment of morals and philosophy. In this they make a bad blunder in reasoning. But then, as I have explained, intellectuals are not very intellectual.

The Arts, exist, as we should put it in our primeval fashion, to show forth the glory of God; or, to translate the same thing in terms of our psychology, to awaken and keep alive the sense of wonder in man. The success of any work of art is achieved when we say of any subject, a tree or a cloud or a human character, "I have seen that a thousand times and I never saw it before. " Now for this purpose a certain variation of VENUE is natural and even necessary. Artists change what they call their attack; for it is to some extent their business to make it a surprise attack. They have to throw a new light on things; and it is not surprising if it is sometimes an invisible ultra-violet ray or one rather resembling a black ray of madness or death. But when the artist extends the eccentric experiment from art to real

32

life, it is quite different. He is like an absent-minded sculptor turning his chisel from chipping at the bust to chipping at the bald head of the distinguished sitter. And these anarchic artists do suffer a little from absence of Mind.

Let us take a practical case for the sake of simplicity. Many moderns will be heard scoffing at what they would call "chocolate-box art"; meaning an insipid and sickly art. And it is easy to call up the sort of picture that might well make anybody ill. I will suppose, for the sake of argument, that we are looking sadly at the outside of a chocolate-box (now, I need hardly say, empty) and that we see painted on it in rather pallid colours a young woman with golden ringlets gazing from a balcony and holding a rose in the spot-light caused by a convenient ray of moonlight. Any similar touches may be added to the taste or distaste of the critic; she may be convulsively clasping a letter or conspicuously wearing an engagement ring or languidly waving farewell to a distant gentleman in a gondola; or anything else I can think of, calculated to cause pain to the sensitive critic. I sympathise with the critic's feeling; but I think he goes quite wrong in his thinking.

Now, what do we mean when we say that this is a silly picture, or a stale subject, or something very difficult to bear, even when we are fortified by chocolates to endure it? We mean it is possible to have too much of a good thing; to have too many chocolate-boxes, as to have too many chocolates. We mean that it is not a picture, but a picture of a picture. Ultimately it is a picture of innumerable pictures; not a real picture of a rose or a girl or a beam of moonlight. In other words, artists have copied artists, right away back to the first sentimental pictures of the Romantic Movement.

But roses have not copied roses. Moonbeams have not imitated each other. And though a woman may copy women in externals, it is only in externals and not in existence; her womanhood was not copied from any other woman. Considered as realities, the rose and the moon and the woman are simply themselves. Suppose that scene to be a real one, and there is nothing particularly imitative about it. The flower is unquestionably fresh as the young woman is unquestionably young. The rose is a real object, which would smell as sweet by any other name, or by no name. The girl is a particular person, whose personality is entirely new to the world and whose experiences are entirely new to herself. If she does indeed choose to stand in that attitude on that balcony holding that botanical specimen (which seems improbable), we have no right to doubt that she has her own reasons for doing so. In short, when once we conceive the thing as reality, we have no reason whatever to dismiss it as mere repetition. So long as we are thinking of the thing as copied mechanically and for money, as a piece of monotonous and mercenary ornament, we naturally feel that the flower is in a special sense an artificial flower and that the moonlight is all moonshine. We feel inclined to welcome even wild variations in the decorative style; and to admire the new artist who will paint the rose black, lest we should forget that it is a deep red, or the moonshine green, that we may realise it is something more subtle than white. But the moon is the moon and the rose is the rose; and we do not expect the real things to alter. Nor is there any reason to expect the rules about them to alter. Nor is there any reason, so far as this question is concerned, to expect the woman to alter her attitude either about the beauty of the rose or the obligations of the engagement-ring. These things, considered as real things, are quite unaffected by the variation of artistic attack in fictitious things. The moon will continue to affect the tides, whether we paint it blue or green or pink with purple spots. And the man who imagines that artistic revolutions must always affect morals is like a man who should say, "I am so bored with seeing pink roses painted on chocolate-boxes that I refuse to believe that roses grow well in a clay soil. "

In short, what the critics would call romanticism is in fact the only form of realism. It is also the only form of rationalism. The more a man uses his reason upon realities, the more he will see that the realities remain much the same, though the representations are very different, And it is only the representations that are repetitions. The sensations are always sincere; the individuals are always individual. If the real girl is experiencing a real romance, she is experiencing something old, but not something stale. If she has plucked something from a real rose-tree, she is holding a very ancient symbol, but a very recent rose. And it is exactly in so far as a man can clear his head, so as to see actual things as they are, that he will see these things as permanently important as they are. Exactly in so far as his head is confused with current fashions and aesthetic modes of the moment, he will see nothing about it except that it is like a picture on a chocolate-box, and not like a picture at the Post-Futurist Gallery. Exactly in so far as he is thinking about real people, he will see that they are really romantic. Exactly in so far as he is thinking only about pictures and poems and decorative styles, he will think that romance is a false or old-fashioned style. He can only see people as imitating pictures; whereas the real people are not imitating anything. They are only being themselves— as they will always be. Roses remain radiant and mysterious, however many pink rosebuds are sprinkled like pips over cheap wallpapers. Falling in love remains radiant and mysterious, however threadbare be the thousandth repetition of a rhyme as a valentine or a cracker-motto. To see this fact is to live in a world of facts. To be always thinking of the banality of bad wallpapers and valentines is to live in a world of fictions.

Now the main truth about all this sceptical revolt, and all the rest of it, is that it was born in a world of fictions. It came from the Intelligentsia, who were perpetually discussing novels and plays and pictures instead of people. They insisted on putting "real life" on the stage and never saw it in the street. They professed to be putting realism into their novels when there was less and less of it in their conversation, as compared with the conversation of the common people. And that perpetual experiment, and shifting of the standpoint, which was natural enough in an artist seeking for certain effects (as it is natural in a photographer hovering round and focussing and fussing with his camera), was wholly inapplicable to any study of the permanent rules and relations of society. When these people began to play about with morals and metaphysics, they simply produced a series of mad worlds where they might have been harmlessly producing a series of mad pictures. Pictures are always meant to catch a certain aspect, at a certain angle, in a certain light; sometimes in light that is almost as brief as lightning. But when the artists became anarchists and began to exhibit the community and the cosmos by these flashes of lightning, the result was not realism but simply nightmare. Because a particular painter, for a particular purpose, might paint the red rose black, the pessimist deduced that the red rose of love and life was really as black as it was painted. Because one artist, from one angle, seized a momentary impression of moonlight as green, the philosopher solemnly put on a pair of green spectacles and declared that it was now a solid scientific certainty that the moon must be crawling with maggots, because it was made of green cheese.

In short, there might have been some value in the old cry of art for the artists; if it had meant that the artists would confine themselves to the medium of art. As a fact, they were always meddling with the medium of morals and religion; and they imported into them the unrest, the changing moods and the merely experimental tricks of their own trade. But a man with a solid sense of reality can see that this is utterly unreal. Whatever the laws of life and love and human relations may be, it is monstrously improbable that they ought to be changed with every fashion in poetry any more than with every fashion in pantaloons. It is insane that there should be a new pattern of hearts or heads whenever there is a new pattern of hats. These things are realities, like a high tide or a clay soil; and you do not get rid of high tides and clay soils by calling roses and moonlight old-fashioned and sentimental. I will venture to say, therefore, and I trust without undue vanity, that I have remained rooted in certain relations and traditions, not because I am a sentimentalist or even a romanticist; but because I am a realist. And I realise that morals must not change with moods, as Cubism must not mean chopping up real houses into cubes, or Vorticism swallowing real ships in whirlpools.

I have not changed my views on these things because there has never been any reason to change them. For anybody impelled by reason and not by running with a crowd will, for instance, perceive that there are always the same arguments for a Purpose and therefore a Personality in things, if he is a thinking person. Only it is now made easy for him to admit vaguely that there may be a Purpose, while denying that there is a Personality, so long as he happens to be a very unthinking person. It is quite as certain as it ever was that life is a gift of God immensely valuable and immensely valued, and anybody can prove it by putting a pistol to the head of a pessimist. Only a certain sort of modern does not like any problem presented to his head; and would dislike a plain question almost as much as a pistol. It is obvious common sense, and obviously consonant to real life, that romantic love is normal to youth and has its natural development in marriage and parenthood as the corresponding conditions of age. None of the nonsense talked about this, that or the other individual irritation or licence has ever made any difference to that solid social truth, for anyone who cares whether things are true, apart from whether they are trite. It is the man who cannot see that a thing is true, although it is trite, who is very truly a victim of mere words and verbal associations. He is the fool who has grown so furious with paper roses that he will not believe that the real rose has a root; nor (till he discovers it with an abrupt and profane ejaculation) that it has a thorn.

The truth is that the modern world has had a mental breakdown; much more than a moral breakdown. Things are being settled by mere associations because there is a reluctance to settle them by arguments. Nearly all the talk about what is advanced and what is antiquated has become a sort of giggling excitement about fashions. The most modern of the moderns stare at a picture of a man making love to a lady in a crinoline with exactly the same sort of vacant grin with which yokels stare at a stranger in an outlandish sort of hat. They regard their fathers of another age exactly as the most insular would regard the foreigners from another country. They seem mentally incapable of getting any further than the statement that our girls are shingled and short-skirted while their silly old great-grandmothers wore ringlets and hoops. That seems to satisfy all their appetite for satire; they are a simple race, a little like savages. They are exactly like the sort of cockney tripper who would roar with laughter because French soldiers wore red trousers and blue coats, while English soldiers were dressed properly in blue trousers and red coats. I have not altered my lines of thought for people who think in this fashion. Why should I?

THE USUAL ARTICLE

THE Editor of an evening paper published recently what he announced as, and even apologized for as "an unusual article. " He anxiously guarded himself from expressing any opinion on the dreadful and dangerous views which the unusual article set forth. Needless to say, before I had read five lines of the unusual article, I knew it was a satisfactory sample of the usual article. It was even a careful and correct copy of the usual article; a sort of prize specimen, as if a thing could be unusually usual. I had read the article before, of course—thousands and thousands of times (as it seems to me)—and had always found it the same; but never before, somehow, had it seemed so exactly the same.

There are things of which the world to-day is subconsciously very weary. It does not always know what they are; for they commonly bear large though faded labels, describing them as the New Movement or the Latest Discovery. For instance, men are already as tired of the Socialist State as if they had been living in it for a thousand years. But there are some things on which boredom is becoming acute. It is now very near the surface; and may suddenly wake up in the form of suicide or murder or tearing newspapers with the teeth. So it is with this familiar product, the Usual Article. It is not only too usual; it has become intolerably, insupportably, unbearably usual. It is appropriately described as "A Woman's Cry to the Churches. " And I beg to announce that, though I am of a heavy and placid habit, and have never been accused of any such feminine graces as hysteria, yet, if I have to read this article three more times, I shall scream. My scream will be entitled, "A Man's Cry to the Newspapers. "

I will repeat somewhat hurriedly what the lady in question cried; for the reader knows it already by heart. The message of Christ was perfectly "simple": that the cure of everything is Love; but since He was killed (I do not quite know why) for making this remark, great temples have been put up to Him and horrid people called priests have given the world nothing but "stones, amulets, formulas, shibboleths. " They also "quarrel eternally among themselves as to the placing of a button or the bending of a knee. " All this gives no comfort to the unhappy Christian, who apparently wishes to be comforted only by being told that he has a duty to his neighbour. "How many men in the time of their passing get comfort out of the thought of the Thirty-Nine Articles, Predestination, Transubstantiation, the doctrine of eternal punishment, and the belief that Christ will return on the Seventh Day? " The items make a curious catalogue; and the last item I find especially mysterious. But I can only say that, if Christ was the giver of the original and really comforting message of love, I should have thought it DID make a difference whether He returned on the Seventh Day. For the rest of that singular list, I should probably find it necessary to distinguish. I certainly never gained any deep and heartfelt consolation from the thought of the Thirty-Nine Articles. I never heard of anybody in particular who did. Of the idea of Predestination there are broadly two views; the Calvinist and the Catholic; and it would make a most uncommon difference to MY comfort, if I held the former instead of the latter. It is the difference between believing that God knows, as a fact, that I choose to go to the devil; and believing that God has given me to the devil, without my having any choice at all. As to Transubstantiation, it is less easy to talk currently about that; but I would gently suggest that, to most ordinary outsiders with any common sense, there would be a considerable practical difference between Jehovah pervading the universe and Jesus Christ coming into the room.

But I touch rapidly and reluctantly on these examples, because they exemplify a much wider question of this interminable way of talking. It consists of talking as if the moral problem of man were perfectly simple, as everyone knows it is not; and then depreciating attempts to solve it by quoting long technical words, and talking about senseless ceremonies without enquiring about their sense. In other words, it is exactly as if somebody were to say about the science of medicine: "All I ask is Health; what could be simpler than the beautiful gift of Health? Why not be content to enjoy for ever the glow of youth and the fresh enjoyment of being fit? Why study dry and dismal sciences of anatomy and physiology; why enquire about the whereabouts of obscure organs of the human body? Why pedantically distinguish between what is labelled a poison and what is labelled an antidote, when it is so simple to enjoy Health? Why worry with a minute exactitude about the number of drops of laudanum or the strength of a dose of chloral, when it is so nice to be healthy? Away with your priestly apparatus of stethoscopes and clinical thermometers; with your ritualistic mummery of feeling pulses, putting out tongues, examining teeth, and the rest! The god Esculapius came on earth solely to inform us that Life is on the whole preferable to Death; and this thought will console many dying persons unattended by doctors. "

In other words, the Usual Article, which is now some ten thousand issues old, was always stuff and nonsense even when it was new. There may be, and there has been, pedantry in the medical profession. There may be, and there has been, theology that was thin or dry or without consolation for men. But to talk as if it were possible for any science to attack any problem, without developing a technical language, and a method always methodical and often minute, merely means that you are a fool and have never really attacked a problem at all. Quite apart from the theory of a Church, if Christ had remained on earth for an indefinite time, trying to induce men to love one another, He would have found it necessary to have some tests, some methods, some way of dividing true love from false love, some way of distinguishing between tendencies that would ruin love and tendencies that would restore it. You cannot make a success of anything, even loving, entirely without thinking. All this is so obvious that it would seem unnecessary to repeat it; and yet it is necessary to repeat it, because it is the flat contradiction of it that is now incessantly repeated. Its flatness stretches around us like a vast wilderness on every side.

It is a character of the Usual Article that it alludes occasionally to the New Religion; but always in a rather timid and remote fashion. It suggests that there will be a better and broader belief; though it seldom touches on the belief, but only on the broadness. There is never in it by any chance anything resembling even the note of the true innovator. For the true innovator must be in some sense a legislator. We may put it in a hostile fashion, by saying that the revolutionist always becomes the tyrant. We may put it in a friendly fashion, by saying that the reformer must return to the idea of form. But anybody really founding a new religion, even a false religion, must have a certain quality of responsibility. He must make himself responsible for saying that some things shall be forbidden and some permitted; that there shall be a certain plan or system that must be defended from destruction. And all the things in any way resembling new religions, to do them justice, do show this quality and suffer this disadvantage. Christian Science is theoretically based on peace and almost on the denial of struggle. But for all that there has been not a little struggle in the councils of that creed; and the relations of all the successors of Mrs. Eddy have by no means been relations of peace. I do not say it as a taunt, but rather as a tribute; I should say that these proceedings did prove that the people involved were trying to found a real religion. It is a compliment to Christian Scientists to say that they also had their tests and their creeds, their anathemas and their excommunications, their encyclicals and their heresy-hunts. But it is a compliment to Christian Scientists which they can hardly use as an insult to Christians. Communism, even in its final form of Marxian materialism, had some of the qualities of a fresh and sincere faith. It had one of them at least; that it did definitely expel men for denying the creed. Both the Communist and the Christian Scientist were under this grave disadvantage; that they did turn a faith into a fact. There is such a thing as a Bolshevist government and it governs, even if it misgoverns. There are such things as Christian Science healers; there probably is such a thing as Christian Science healing, even if we do not fully admit that the healing is health. There is a Church in active operation; and for that reason it exhibits all the dogmas and differences charged against the Church of Christ. But the philosophy expressed in the Usual Article avoids all these disadvantages by never coming into the world of reality at all. Its god is afraid to be born; its scripture is afraid to be written; it only manages to remain as the New Religion by always coming to-morrow and never to-day. It puffs itself out with spiritual pride, because it does not impose what it cannot even invent. It shines with Pharisaical self-satisfaction, because there are no crimes committed for its creed and no creed to be the motive of its crimes. This sort of critic is a surgeon who never performs an unsuccessful operation because he never operates; a soldier who never falls because he never fights. Anybody can talk for ever about a non-existent religion which shall be free from all the evils of existence. Anybody can dream of that entirely humane and harmonious Christianity, whose Christ is never born and never crucified. It is so easy to do, that half a hundred people in the papers and the public discussions have been doing nothing else for the last twenty or thirty years. But it is every bit as futile as applied to a spiritual ideal as it would be if applied to a scientific theory or a political programme; and I only mention it because I have just heard it for the hundredth time; and feel a faint hope that I may be mentioning it for the last time.

WHY I AM A CATHOLIC

A LEADING article in a daily paper was recently devoted to the New Prayer Book; without having anything very new to say about it. For it mostly consisted in repeating for the nine-hundredth-and-ninety-nine-thousandth time that what the ordinary Englishman wants is a religion without dogma (whatever that may be), and that the disputes about Church matters were idle and barren on both sides. Only, suddenly remembering that this equalisation of both sides might possibly involve some slight concession or consideration for our side, the writer hastily corrected himself. He proceeded to suggest that though it is wrong to be dogmatic, it is essential to be dogmatically Protestant. He suggested that the ordinary Englishman (that useful character) was quite convinced, in spite of his aversion to all religious differences, that it was vital to religion to go on differing from Catholicism. He is convinced (we were told) that "Britain is as Protestant as the sea is salt. " Gazing reverently at the profound Protestantism of Mr. Michael Arlen or Mr. Noel Coward, or the latest jazz dance in Mayfair, we might be tempted to ask: If the salt lose its savour, wherewith shall it be salted? But since we may rightly deduce from this passage that Lord Beaverbrook and Mr. James Douglas and Mr. Hannen Swaffer, and all their following, are indeed stern and unbending Protestants (and as we know that Protestants are famous for the close and passionate study of the Scriptures, unhindered by Pope or priest), we might even take the liberty of interpreting the saying in the light of a less familiar text. Is it possible that in comparing Protestantism to the salt of the sea they were haunted with some faint memory of another passage, in which the same Authority spoke of one single and sacred fountain that is of living water, because it is of life-giving water, and really quenches the thirst of men; while all other pools and puddles are distinguished from it by the fact that those who drink of them will thirst again. It is a thing that does occasionally happen to people who prefer to drink salt water.

This is perhaps a somewhat provocative way of opening the statement of my strongest conviction; but I would respectfully plead that the provocation came from the Protestant. When Protestantism calmly claims to rule all the souls in the tone of Britannia ruling all the seas, it is permissible to retort that the very quintessence of such salt can be found thickest in the stagnation of the Dead Sea. But it is still more permissible to retort that Protestantism is claiming what no religion at this moment can possibly claim. It is calmly claiming the allegiance of millions of agnostics, atheists, hedonistic pagans, independent mystics, psychic investigators, theists, theosophists, followers of Eastern cults and jolly fellows living like the beasts that perish. To pretend that all these are Protestants is considerably to lower the prestige and significance of Protestantism. It is to make it merely negative; and salt is not negative.

Taking this as a text and test of the present problem of religious choice, we find ourselves faced from the first with a dilemma about the traditional religion of our fathers. Protestantism as here named is either a negative or a positive thing. If Protestantism is a positive thing, there is no doubt whatever that it is dead. In so far as it really was a set of special spiritual beliefs it is no longer believed. The genuine Protestant creed is now hardly held by anybody—least of all by the Protestants. So completely have they lost faith in it, that they have mostly forgotten what it was. If almost any modern man be asked whether we save our souls solely through our theology, or whether doing good (to the poor, for instance) will help us on the road to God, he would answer without hesitation that good works are probably more pleasing to God than theology. It would probably come as quite a surprise to him to learn that, for three hundred years, the faith in faith alone was the badge of a Protestant, the faith in good works the rather shameful badge of a disreputable Papist. The ordinary Englishman (to bring in our old friend once more) would now be in no doubt whatever on the merits of the long quarrel between Catholicism and Calvinism. And that was the most important and intellectual quarrel between Catholicism and Protestantism. If he believes in a God at all, or even if he does not, he would quite certainly prefer a God who has made all men for joy, and desires to save them all, to a God who deliberately made some for involuntary sin and immortal misery. But that was the quarrel; and it was the Catholic who held the first and the Protestant who held the second. The modern man not only does not share, he does not even understand, the unnatural aversion of the Puritans to all art and beauty in relation to religion. Yet that was the real Protestant protest; and right into the Mid-Victorian time Protestant matrons were shocked at a white gown, let alone a coloured vestment. On practically every essential count on which the Reformation actually put Rome in the dock, Rome has since been acquitted by the jury of the whole world.

It Is perfectly true that we can find real wrongs, provoking rebellion, in the Roman Church just before the Reformation. What we cannot find is one ot those real wrongs that the Reformation reformed. For instance, it was an abominable abuse that the corruption of the monasteries sometimes permitted a rich noble to play the patron and even play at being the Abbot, or draw on the revenues supposed to belong to a brotherhood of poverty and charity. But all that the Reformation did was to allow the same rich noble to take over ALL the revenue, to seize the whole house and turn it into a palace or a pig-sty, and utterly stamp out the last legend of the poor brotherhood. The worst things in worldly Catholicism were made worse by Protestantism. But the best things remained somehow through the era of corruption; nay, they survived even the era of reform. They survive to-day in all Catholic countries, not only in the colour and poetry and popularity of religion, but in the deepest lessons of practical psychology. And so completely are they justified, after the judgment of four centuries, that every one of them is now being copied, even by those who condemned it; only it is often caricatured. Psycho-analysis is the Confessional without the safeguards of the Confessional; Communism is the Franciscan movement without the moderating balance of the Church; and American sects, having howled for three centuries at the Popish theatricality and mere appeal to the senses, now "brighten" their services by super-theatrical films and rays of rose-red light falling on the head of the minister. If we had a ray of light to throw about, we should not throw it on the minister.

Next, Protestantism may be a negative thing. In other words, it may be a new and totally different list of charges against Rome; and only in continuity because it is still against Rome. That is very largely what it is; and that is presumably what the DAILY EXPRESS really meant, when it said that our country and our countrymen are soaked in Protestantism as in salt. In other words, the legend that Rome is wrong anyhow, is still a living thing, though all the features of the monster are now entirely altered in the caricature. Even this is an exaggeration, as applied to the England of to-day; but there is still a truth in it. Only the truth, when truly realised, can hardly be very satisfactory to honest and genuine Protestants. For, after all, what sort of a tradition is this, that tells a different story every day or every decade, and is content so long as all the contradictory tales are told against one man or one institution? What sort of holy cause is it to inherit from our ancestors, that we should go on hating something and being consistent only in hatred; being fickle and false in everything else, even in our reason for hating it? Are we really to settle down seriously to make up a new set of stories against the bulk of our fellow-Christians? Is that Protestantism; and is that worth comparing to patriotism or the sea?

Anyhow, that was the situation I found myself facing when I began to think of these things, the child of a purely Protestant ancestry and, in the ordinary sense, of a Protestant household. But as a fact my family, having become Liberal, was no longer Protestant. I was brought up a sort of Universalist and Unitarian; at the feet of that admirable man, Stopford Brooke. It was not Protestantism save in a very negative sense. Often it was the flat contrary of Protestantism, even in that sense. For instance, the Universalist did not believe in hell; and he was emphatic in saying that heaven was a happy state of mind—"a temper." But he had the sense to see that most men do not live or die in a state of mind so happy that it will alone ensure them a heaven. If heaven is a temper, it is certainly not a universal temper; and a good many people pass through this life in a devil of a temper. If all these were to have heaven, solely through happiness, it seemed clear that something must happen to them first. The Universalist therefore believed in a progress after death, at once punishment and enlightenment. In other words, he believed in Purgatory; though he did not believe in Hell. Right or wrong, he obviously and flatly contradicted the Protestant, who believed in Hell but not in Purgatory. Protestantism, through its whole history, had waged ceaseless war on this one idea of Purgatory or Progress beyond the grave. I have come to see in the complete Catholic view much deeper truths on all three ideas; truths concerned with will and creation and God's most glorious love of liberty. But even at the start, though I had no thought of Catholicism, I could not see why I should have any concern with Protestantism; which had always said the very opposite of what a Liberal is now expected to say.

I found, in plain words, that there was no longer any question of clinging to the Protestant faith. It was simply a question of whether I should cling to the Protestant feud. And to my enormous astonishment, I found a large number of my fellow Liberals eager to go on with the Protestant feud, though they no longer held the Protestant faith. I have no title to judge them; but to me, I confess, it seemed like a rather ugly breach of honour. To find out that you have been slandering somebody about something, to refuse to apologise, and to make up another more plausible story against him, so that you can carry on the spirit of the slander, seemed to me at the start a rather poor way of behaving. I resolved at least to consider the original slandered institution on its own merits and the first and most obvious question was: Why were Liberals so very illiberal about it? What was the meaning of the feud, so constant and so inconsistent? That question took a long time to answer and would now take much too long a time to record. But it led me at last to the only logical answer, which every fact of life now confirms; that the thing is hated, as nothing else is hated, simply because it is, in the exact sense of the popular phrase, like nothing on earth.

There is barely space here to indicate this one thing out of the thousand things that confirm the same fact and confirm each other. I would undertake to pick up any topic at random, from pork to pyrotechnics, and show that it illustrates the truth of the only true philosophy; so realistic is the remark that all roads lead to Rome. Out of all these I have here only taken one fact; that the thing is pursued age after age by an unreasonable hatred that is perpetually changing its reason. Now of nearly all the dead heresies it may be said that they are not only dead, but damned; that is, they are condemned or would be condemned by common sense, even outside the Church, when once the mood and mania of them is passed. Nobody now wants to revive the Divine Right of Kings which the first Anglicans advanced against the Pope. Nobody now wants to revive the Calvinism which the first Puritans advanced against the King. Nobody now is sorry that the Iconoclasts were prevented from smashing all the statues of Italy. Nobody now is sorry that the Jansenists failed to destroy all the dramas of France. Nobody who knows anything about the Albigensians regrets that they did not convert the world to pessimism and perversion. Nobody who really understands the logic of the Lollards (a much more sympathetic set of people) really wishes that they had succeeded in taking away all political rights and privileges from everybody who was not in a state of grace. "Dominion founded on Grace" was a devout ideal, but considered as a plan for disregarding an Irish policeman controlling the traffic in Piccadilly, until we have discovered whether he has confessed recently to his Irish priest, it is wanting in actuality. In nine cases out of ten the Church simply stood for sanity and social balance against heretics who were sometimes very like lunatics. Yet at each separate moment the pressure of the prevalent error was very strong; the exaggerated error of a whole generation, like the strength of the Manchester School in the 'fifties, or of Fabian Socialism as a fashion in my own youth. A study of the true historical cases commonly shows us the spirit of the age going wrong, and the

Catholics at least relatively going right. It is a mind surviving a hundred moods.

As I say, this is only one aspect; but it was the first that affected me and it leads on to others. When a hammer has hit the right nail on the head a hundred times, there comes a time when we think it was not altogether by accident. But these historical proofs would be nothing without the human and personal proofs, which would need quite a different sort of description. It is enough to say that those who know the Catholic practice find it not only right, but always right when everything else is wrong; making the Confessional the very throne of candour where the world outside talks nonsense about it as a sort of conspiracy; upholding humility when everybody is praising pride; charged with sentimental charity when the world is talking a brutal utilitarianism; charged with dogmatic harshness when the world is loud and loose with vulgar sentimentalism—as it is to-day. At the place where the roads meet there is no doubt of the convergence. A man may think all sorts of things, most of them honest and many of them true, about the right way to turn in the maze at Hampton Court. But he does not think he is in the centre; he knows.

WHAT DO THEY THINK?

ALL science, even the divine science, is a sublime detective story. Only it is not set to detect why a man is dead; but the darker secret of why he is alive. The Catholic Church remains in the best sense a mystery even to believers. It would be foolish of them to complain if it is a riddle to unbelievers. But in a more practical sense we may well ask a question. What do they think it really is? What do they think we think it really is? What do they think it is all about, or even supposed to be all about? That problem becomes darker and darker for me, the more I stare at it. It becomes black as midnight, for instance, when I stare at such a sentence as I saw recently in TRUTH, a singularly intelligent and often a highly valuable paper. It stated that Rome tolerates, in her relation with the Russian Uniats, "strange heresies and even bearded and wedded clergy. "

In that one extraordinary phrase, what formless monster begins to take form in their visions? In those eight words it is not too much to say that every term is startling in its inconsequence. As somebody tumbling down the stairs bumps upon every step, the writer comes a crash upon every word. The word "strange" is strange enough. The word "heresy" is stranger. Perhaps at first sight the word "bearded, " with its joyous reminiscences of the game of Beaver, may appear the most funny. "Wedded" is also funny. Even the "and" between bearded and wedded is funny. But by far the funniest and most fantastic thing in all that fantastic sentence is the word "even. "

It is not everybody who can thus bestrew a page with comic conjunctions and farcical particles of speech. Only a wild unreason, about the whole way the thing hangs together, could thus make even the joints and hinges of that rickety statement rattle and creak with laughter. We can hardly say of this version of the Roman Catholic faith that it is a false version, or that it differs from the true version, or even that it differs from our version. What is the version; and how can it be even their version? There is in the world, they would tell us, a powerful and persecuting superstition, intoxicated with the impious idea of having a monopoly of divine truth, and therefore cruelly crushing and exterminating everything else as error. It burns thinkers for thinking, discoverers for discovering, philosophers and theologians who differ by a hair's breadth from its dogmas; it will tolerate no tiny change or shadow of variety even among its friends and followers; it sweeps the whole world with one encyclical cyclone of uniformity; it would destroy nations and empires for a word, so wedded is it to its fixed idea that its own word is the Word of God. When it is thus sweeping the world, it comes to a remote and rather barbarous region somewhere on the borders of Russia; where it stops suddenly; smiles broadly; and tells the people there that they can have the strangest heresies they like. Strange heresies, by the standard of strangeness likely to exist in an experience so long as that of the Roman Church, may well be very strange indeed. The Church is no stranger to heresies that involved human sacrifice, or the worship of demons, or the practice of perversions. We might well suppose, therefore, that the Church says benevolently to these fortunate Slavs, "By all means worship Baphomet and Beelzebub; say the Lord's Prayer backwards; continue to drink the blood of infants — nay, even, " and here her voice falters, till she rallies with an effort of generous resolution, " — yes, even, if you really must, grow a beard. " And then, I suppose, we must call up yet darker and more dreadful visions, of the heretic hiding himself in secret places, in caverns of witchcraft or sealed gardens of black magic, while the blasphemous beard is grown. Nobody explains why these particular Eastern Europeans should be regarded with so much favour, or why a number of long hairs on the chin should be regarded with so much disfavour. It is presumably a problem on which this intolerant spiritual tyranny will suffer no question to be asked.

Does the reader realise the despair that falls upon the hapless Catholic journalist at such moments; or how wild a prayer he may well send up for the intercession of St. Francis of Sales? What is he to say; or at what end of that sentence is he to begin? What is the good of his laboriously beginning to explain that a married clergy is a matter of discipline and not doctrine, that it can therefore be allowed locally without heresy — when all the time the man thinks a beard as important as a wife and more important than a false religion? What is the sense of explaining to him the peculiar historical circumstances that have led to preserving some local habits in Kiev or Warsaw, when the man at any moment may receive a mortal shock by seeing a bearded Franciscan walking through Wimbledon or Walham Green? What we want to get at is the mind of the man who can think so absurdly about us as to suppose we could have a horror of heresy, and then a weakness for heresy, and then a greater horror of hair. To what does he attribute all the inconsistent nonsense and inconsequent bathos that he associates with us? Does he think we are all joking; or all dreaming; or all out of our minds; or what does he think? Until we have got at that, we have really got very little further.

The notion that he merely thinks the Church is all nonsense is not very consistent with the way in which he talks about her in other aspects; as when he says she has always resisted such and such changes, which he perhaps approves; or that she can be counted on as an influence for such and such principles, which he perhaps dislikes; or that she is forbidden to accept this doctrine or committed to defending that. But what he can possibly suppose to be the principle upon which she accepts or rejects doctrines I never can imagine. And the more we really come in contact with the puzzle, the more we shall feel, I think, something quite unique and even creepy about it. It is like the old fable of the five blind men who tried to explore an elephant; a fable that used to be told as a sort of farce; but which I can well imagine being told by Maeterlinck or some modern mystic so as to make the flesh creep with mysteries. The thing is at once so obvious and so invisible; so public and so impalpable; so universal and so secret. They say so much about it; and they say so little. They see so much of it; and they see so little. There is a sort of colossal contradiction, such as can only be conceived between different dimensions or different planes of thought, in the coexistence of such familiar fact and such utterly unknown truth. Indeed, there is only one combination of words I know of, which ever did exactly express so huge a human and historical paradox; and they also are familiar and unfathomable: "The light shone in the darkness and the darkness comprehended it not. "

Some part of the difficulty is doubtless due to the odd way in which so many people are at once preoccupied with it and prejudiced against it. It is queer to observe so much ignorance with so little indifference. They love talking about it and they hate hearing about it. It would seem that they especially hate asking about it. If, for instance, a man contributing to TRUTH, in the middle of educated London, really were a little puzzled by Rome making an exception of the Uniats, and were perhaps especially puzzled by an exception to the celibacy of the clergy (I omit his dark and inscrutable broodings on the subject of Beavers) might it not have occurred to him to go and ask some Catholic priest, or for that matter, some Catholic layman, and thus gain some sort of rough idea of the relative importance attached in our system to celibacy and heresy and hair on the face? Could he not have gained a glimpse of the usual order or hierarchy of these ideas, which would have prevented him from writing the staggering word "and" or the stunning word "even"? But I am inclined to suspect that even this omission, negative as it may seem, has in it something deeper than mere negligence. I fancy that there is more than meets the eye in this curious controversial attitude; the desire to ask rhetorical questions and not to ask real questions; the wish to heckle and not to hear. It may well be connected with more mystical aspects of the whole question, on which I am certainly not going to speculate, since they are admittedly the most subtle problems of the trained theologian; all those questions about the will to believe and the operations of grace; and the fact that something more than reason is needed to bring any of us into the most reasonable of all philosophies.

But apart from these mysteries, I think there is another reason that is human and historical. The thing that causes Catholic philosophy to be neglected is the very thing that really makes it impossible to neglect. It is the fact that it was something left for dead; and now rather incredibly come to life. An ordinary man would not mind very much whether he knew the exact ritual with which Roman augurs examined the entrails of beasts or watched the movements of birds; because he is certain that the world will not go back to that Roman religion. The world was once almost as certain that it would not go back to this other Roman religion. A man would not be very much ashamed of having put the metals in the wrong order in the imaginary formula of an alchemist, described in a historical romance; because he is convinced that alchemists can only return in romance and can never return in history. There was a time when he felt quite as safe about abbots as about alchemists. That time has already passed. That mere confident contempt, as I have said, has already been succeeded by a rather restless curiosity. But mental habits overlap; and the dead momentum of the old disregard of facts goes along side by side with a new movement of anxiety about possibilities. They would not be so ignorant about it if they had not decided that it was dead. They would not be so irritated about it if they had not discovered that it was alive. For ignorance accumulates like knowledge; and these newly aroused critics are the inheritors of the accruing interest of four hundred years of an ignorance that became an indifference. At this moment they are no longer indifferent; but they are still ignorant. They have been awakened suddenly in the watches of the night, and what they see they can neither deny nor understand. For they see one that was dead walking; and the blaze of that living death blasts or obliterates all the older details of life; and all the fables they have believed and all the facts they have forgotten are alike swallowed up in the miracle they can neither believe nor forget.

THE MASK OF THE AGNOSTIC

SIR ARTHUR KEITH, in his recent remarks on the soul, let the cat out of the bag. He let it out of that very prim and proper professional bag which is carried by the "medical man" whom he described as conscientiously compelled to assert that the life of the soul ceases with the breath of the body. Perhaps the figure which fits in so well with the bag is less fortunate in the case of the cat; a mystic animal, whose nine lives might rather be supposed to represent immortality, at least in the form of reincarnation. But anyhow, he let the cat out of the bag; in the sense of revealing a secret which such wise men would be wiser to keep. It is the secret that such scientists do not speak as scientists, but simply as materialists. That is, they do not give their conclusions, but simply their opinions; and a very shaky sort of opinions some of them are.

Not long ago, in his famous address on Anthropoids to the Congress at Leeds, Sir Arthur Keith said that he spoke simply as the foreman of a jury. It is true that he had not apparently consulted the jury; and it was rapidly made clear that the jury violently disagreed; which is unusual in a jury after the foreman has delivered the verdict. Still, in using this image he meant to claim complete impartiality of a judicial sort. He meant that a juryman is bound by oath to go entirely by the facts and the evidence, without fear or favour. And this effect would be a hundred times more effective if we were left free to imagine that the juryman's personal sympathies might be on the other side; or at least, if we did not know that they were very keenly on the one side. Sir Arthur should have been careful to preserve the impression that, speaking strictly and solely as an anthropologist, he was forced to accept the natural selection of anthropoids. He should then have left it to be inferred that, merely as a private person, he might be yearning for seraphic visions and celestial hopes; he might be searching the Scriptures or awaiting the Apocalypse. For all it was any business of ours, or any business of anybody's, he might be in private life a Mormon multiplying the stars in his heavenly crown or a Holy Roller continually convulsed by the Holy Ghost. The point was that the facts forced the Darwinian conclusion upon him. And a man of that sort, being forced to accept them, would be a real witness because a reluctant witness. In the trial of Darwin the man might feel for the plaintiff, but the juryman would be forced to find for the defendant.

And now Sir Arthur Keith has thrown the whole of that imperial impartiality away. He has gone out of his way to dogmatise and lay down the law about the soul; which has nothing to do with his subject, except in so far as it is everybody's subject. But while it does not relate to what is his subject, it has told everybody which is his side. It has turned the foreman of the jury into a very unmistakable advocate for that side. Indeed, such a partisan is more like a party to the suit than an advocate; since it is the whole point that as a private person he has long had the private prejudice. Henceforth it is obvious that Keith deciding for Darwin is simply like Bradlaugh deciding for Darwin, or Ingersoll deciding for Darwin, or any atheist on a stool in Hyde Park deciding for Darwin. When THEY choose the side of natural selection, we can all agree that it is a very natural selection.

As to the conclusion itself, it seems almost incredibly inconclusive. Unless Sir Arthur Keith is very badly misreported, he specially stated that spiritual existence ceases with the physical functions; and that no medical man could conscientiously say anything else. However grave be the injury called death (which indeed is often fatal), this strikes me as a case in which it is quite unnecessary to call in a medical man at all. There is always a certain irony, even in the simple pages of my favourite detective stories, in the fact that everybody rushes for a doctor as soon as they are quite certain that a man is dead. But in the detective story there may at least be something to be learnt by the doctor from the dead body. In the doctrinal speculation there is nothing whatever; and it does but confuse the eternal detective story for the doctor of medicine to pretend to be a doctor of divinity. The truth is that all this business about "a medical man" is mere bluff and mystagogy. The medical man "sees" that the mind has ceased with the body. What the medical man sees is that the body can no longer kick, talk, sneeze, whistle or dance a jig. And a man does not need to be very medical in order to see that. But whether the principle of energy, that once made it kick, talk, sneeze, whistle and dance, does or does not still exist on some other plane of existence— a medical man knows no more about that than any other man. And when medical men were clear-headed, some of them (like an ex-surgeon named Thomas Henry Huxley) said they did not believe that medical men or any men could know anything about it. That is an intelligible position; but it does not seem to be Sir Arthur Keith's position. He has been put up publicly to DENY that the soul survives the body; and to make the extraordinary remark that any medical man must say the same. It is as if we were to say that any competent builder or surveyor must deny the possibility of the Fourth Dimension; because he has learnt the technical secret that a building is measured by length, breadth and height. The obvious query is—Why bring in a surveyor? Everybody knows that everything is in fact measured by three dimensions. Anybody who thinks there is a fourth dimension thinks so in spite of being well aware that things are generally measured by three. Or it is as if a man were to answer a Berkeleian metaphysician, who holds all matter to be an illusion of mind, by saying, "I can call the evidence of an intelligent navvy who actually has to deal with solid concrete and cast iron; and he will tell you they are quite real." We should naturally answer that we do not need a navvy to tell us that solid things are solid; and it is quite in another sense that the philosopher says they are not solid. Similarly, there is nothing to make a medical man a materialist, except what might make any man a materialist. And it is when a man has absorbed all that obvious materialism that he begins to use his mind. And, as some hold, does not stop.

This very unphilosophical irruption into philosophy was, however, in one way enlightening. It threw a light backwards on the speaker's previous proclamation on things on which he has more right to speak. Even in those things he betrayed a curious simplicity common among such official scientists. The truth is that they become steadily less scientific and more official. They develop that thin disguise that is the daily wear of politicians. They perform before us the most artful tricks with the most artless transparency. It is like watching a child trying to hide something. They are perpetually trying to bluff us with big words and learned allusions; on the assumption that we have never learnt anything—even of their own funny little ways. Every leader-writer who thunders "Galileo" at us assumes that we know even less about Galileo than he does. Every preacher of popular science who throws a long word at us thinks we shall have to look it up in the dictionary and hopes we shall not study it seriously even in the encyclopaedia. Their use of science is rather like the use made of it by the heroes of certain adventure stories, in which the white men terrify the savages by predicting an eclipse or producing an electric shock. These are in a sense true demonstrations of science. They are in a sense right in saying that they are scientists. Where they are perhaps wrong is in supposing that we are savages.

But it is rather amusing for us who watch the preparations for giving us an electric shock, when we are seriously expected to be shocked by the shock. It is rather a joke when we, the benighted savages, are ourselves not only quite capable of predicting the eclipse, but capable of predicting the prediction. Now, among these facts that have been familiar to us for a long time is the fact that men of science stage and prepare their effects exactly as politicians do. They also do it rather badly—exactly as politicians do. Neither of these two modern mystagogues has yet realised how transparent his tricks have become. One of the most familiar and transparent of them is what is known as the "official contradiction. " It is a strange symbolic way of declaring that something has happened by denying that it has happened. So whitewashing reports are published after political scandals as regularly as bluebooks. So the Right Honourable Gentleman hopes it is not necessary for him to contradict what he feels sure the Honourable Member could not have intended to insinuate. So a Cabinet Minister is put up to deny from a platform that there is any change in the Government's policy about Damascus. And so Sir Arthur Keith is put up to deny that there is any change in the scientific attitude about Darwin.

And when we hear that, we all give a sort of sigh of satisfaction; for we all know exactly what THAT means. It means more or less the opposite of what it says. It means that there has been a devil of a row about Damascus inside the Party, or, in other words, that there is beginning to be a devil of a scandal about discredited Darwinians inside the scientific world. The curious thing is that in the latter case the officials are not only solemn in uttering the official contradiction, but much more simple in supposing that nobody will realize that it is official. In the case of the similar legal fiction in politics, the politicians by this time not only know the truth, but often know that we know the truth. Everybody knows by this time, by the gossip that is repeated everywhere, exactly what is meant by the absolute agreement on everything which binds the Prime Minister and all his colleagues. The Prime Minister does not really expect us to believe that he is the holy and beloved king of a brotherhood of knights sworn to a faith and giving their hearts to him alone. But Sir Arthur Keith does really expect us to believe that he is the foreman of a jury containing all the different men of science, all absolutely agreed that Darwin's particular opinion was "eternal. " That is what I mean by childish concealment; and the artless or transparent trick. That is why I say that they do not even know how much we know.

For the politician is less pompously absurd than the anthropologist, even if we test it by what they both call Progress; which is mostly only another word for Time. We all know the official optimism which always defends the present government. But this is like an official defence of all the past governments. If a man were to say that the politics of Palmerston were eternal, we should think him a little out of date. Yet Darwin was prominent at about the same date as Palmerston; and is quite equally dated. If Mr. Lloyd George were to get up and say that the great Liberal Party had not receded from one single position taken up by Gobden and Bright, the only true Tribunes of the People, we should reluctantly conclude (if such a thing be conceivable) that he was talking party claptrap to people ignorant of the history of the party. If a social reformer were to affirm solemnly that all social philosophy was still proceeding strictly on the principles of Herbert Spencer, we should know it was doing nothing of the sort, and that only an absolutely fossilized official could pretend that it was. Yet Darwin and Spencer were not only contemporaries but comrades and allies; and the Darwinian biology and the Spencerian sociology were regarded as parts of the same movement, which our grandfathers regarded as a very modern movement. Even considered a priori as a matter of probability it therefore seems rather unlikely that the science of that generation was any more infallible than its ethics and politics. Even on the principles Sir Arthur professes, it seems very queer that there should now be no more to be said about Darwinism than he said about it. But we do not need to appeal to those principles or those probabilities. We can appeal to the facts. As it happens, we do know something about the facts; and Sir Arthur Keith does not seem to know that we know.

It was in a Catholic paper that certain statements were made about Darwinism to-day; statements which Sir Arthur Keith himself went out of his way to contradict; and about which Sir Arthur Keith himself was proved sensationally and disastrously wrong. Probably the story is now known to all readers of that paper; but it will possibly never come to the knowledge of most other journalists, and it certainly will not be recorded in most of the other papers. Touching this cosmic controversy, most of the other papers are emphatically party papers; and they support the party leader when he publishes the official contradiction. They will not let the public know how triumphantly his other contradiction was contradicted.

When Mr. Belloc stated that these Darwinians were out of date and ignorant of recent biology, he quoted among a great many other recent authorities the French biologist Vialleton as denying the possibility of natural selection in a particular case connected with reptiles and birds. Sir Arthur Keith, coming to the rescue of Mr. H. G. Wells, and eager to prove that he and Mr. Wells were not out of date or ignorant of recent biology, proceeded to contradict Mr. Belloc flatly. He said that there was no such statement in Vialleton's book; in other words, he accused Mr. Belloc of having misquoted or misrepresented Vialleton's book. It then appeared, to the amazement of everybody, and especially of Mr. Belloc, that Sir Arthur Keith did not even know of the existence of the book. He was referring only to an early and elementary work by the same author published long ago. That was the last he had ever read of Vialleton. The important book, of which even I, a mere unscientific man in the street, had heard at least something, had never come to his ears at all. In short, the general charge, that Darwinians are out of date in their information, was proved about as completely as anything controversial can ever be proved in this world.

Now, when a thing like that has happened, above all when it has happened to us, in the pages of a paper in which I write, in the experience of one of my own friends, how can it be expected that people in our position should take seriously the speech at the opening of the British Association at Leeds? How can we keep a straight face when the President strikes an attitude as if pointing to the stars and declaring Darwinism equally eternal? That sort of thing is not meant for us; but for the reporters; just as the true story of Wells and Belloc is generally kept out of the reports.

THE EARLY BIRD IN HISTORY

ST. JOAN OF ARC, a star and a thunderbolt, strange as a meteoric stone whose very solidity is not of this earth, may be compared also to a diamond among pebbles; the one white stone of history. Like a diamond, she is clear but not simple, as some count simplicity; but having many facets or aspects. There is one aspect of the discussion on St. Joan which I have never seen specially noted, and it seems to be worth a note. It concerns that common and current charge against the Catholic Church that she is, as the phrase goes, always behind the times.

When I became a Catholic, I was quite prepared to find that in many respects she really was behind the times. I was very tolerant of the idea of being behind the times, having had long opportunities of studying the perfectly ghastly people who were abreast of the times; or the still more pestilent people who were in advance of the times. I was prepared to find Catholicism rather Conservative, and in that sense slow; and so, of course, in some aspects it is. I knew that being in the movement generally meant only being in the fashion. I knew that fashions had an extraordinary way of being first omnipresent and oppressive and then suddenly blank and forgotten. I knew how publicity seems fixed like a spotlight and vanishes like a lightning-flash. I had seen the whole public imagination filled with a succession of Krugers and Kaisers, who were to be hanged next week and about whom nobody cared a hang next month. I have lived through an overwhelming illusion that there was nobody in the world except General Gordon or Captain Dreyfus or the elephant Jumbo at the Zoo. If there is something in the world that takes no notice of these world-changes, I confess to finding a certain comfort in its indifference. I think it was just as well, from every point of view, that the ecclesiastical authorities delayed a decision about Darwinism or even Evolution; and declined altogether to be excited in that universal excitement. There were many, even among the sympathetic, who seemed to think that Catholics ought to put up an altar to the Missing Link, as Pagans did to the Unknown God. But Catholics prefer to wait until they know what they are doing; and would prefer to learn a little more about a thing besides the fact that nobody can find it. And of course it is true that in some matters, judged by the feverish pace of recent fashion, the Church has always been slow as well as sure. But there is another side of the truth, and one which is more commonly missed. As it happens, both sides are strikingly illustrated in the story of the status of St. Joan.

If we go back to the very beginning of a story, we very often find that the Church did actually do something which her foes ignored and even her friends forgot. Then other social tendencies set in, other questions occupied the world, the tides of time and change passed over the whole business; and when that business came again to the surface, the world had the impression that the Church was dealing with it after a very long delay. But the world itself had never dealt with it at all. The world, as a matter of fact, had never woken up to the fact at all, until it woke up with a start and began to abuse the Church for not having woken up before. During all those long intervening ages, the world had really been much more asleep than the Church. The Church, a very long time ago, had done something; and the world had done nothing. The case of St. Joan of Arc is one curious example.

The Canonisation of St. Joan came very slowly and very late. But the Rehabilitation of St. Joan came very promptly and very early. It is a very exceptional example of rapid reparation for a judicial crime or a miscarriage of justice. There have been any number of these judicial crimes in history. There have been any number of heroes and martyrs whom history regards as having suffered for their virtues. It has almost passed into a popular proverb, especially in modern times; as in the words of the American popular poet: "Right for ever on the scaffold, wrong for ever on the throne. " But I can hardly remember another example of the throne paying so prompt a salute to the scaffold. The condemnation of St. Joan was reversed by the Pope in the lifetime of her contemporaries, at the appeal of her brothers; about as soon as anybody could have expected anything of the sort to be reversed. I do not know if the Athenian Republic did as much for Socrates or the Florentine for Savonarola; but I am pretty certain that nobody could have got the Carthaginians to apologise thus to Regulus or the Antiochi to Maccabaeus. The only really fair way of considering the fashionable subject of the crimes of Christendom would be to compare them with the crimes of heathenism; and the normal human practice of the Pagan world. And while it may be a weakness of human beings, of every age and creed, to stone the prophets and then build their sepulchres, it is really very seldom that the sepulchre is built even as quickly as that. When those who build the sepulchre are really and truly the representatives or inheritors of those who threw the stones, it does not generally happen for hundreds of years. To take the parallel passions of the secular side of the Middle Ages, we should be considerably surprised to learn that when the head of William Wallace had been stuck on a spike by Edward the First, his remains had been respectfully interred and his character cleared by Edward the Third. We should be considerably surprised if the courts of Queen Elizabeth had gone out of their way to repudiate and quash the case against Thomas More. It is generally long afterwards, when the actual ambitions and rivalries are dead, when the feuds and family interests have long been forgotten, that a rather sentimental though sincere tenderness is shown to the dead enemy. In the nineteenth century the English do make a romance about Wallace and a statue of Washington. In the nineteenth and twentieth centuries the English do produce a fine enthusiasm and a number of excellent books about St. Joan. And I for one hope to see the day when this measure of magnanimity shall be filled up where it has been most wanting; and some such payment made for the deepest debt of all. I should like to see the day when the English put up a statue of Emmett beside the statue of Washington; and I wish that in the Centenary of Emancipation there were likely to be as much fuss in London about the figure of Daniel O'Connell as there was about that of Abraham Lincoln.

But I mean the comment here in a rather larger sense; and in a larger sense it is an even stronger case. I mean that if we take the tale of St. Joan as a test, the really remarkable thing is not so much the slowness of the Church to appreciate her, as the slowness of everybody else. The world, especially the wisest men of the world, were extraordinarily late in realising what a remarkable thing had happened; very much later than the rather rigid religious officials of the fifteenth century. That rigidity of fifteenth century religion was very soon broken up, partly by good and partly by bad forces. Comparatively soon after St. Joan's ashes were thrown into the Seine, quite soon after the Rehabilitation, the Renaissance had really begun. Very soon after that the Reformation had begun. The Renaissance produced a number of large and liberal views on all sorts of things. The Reformation produced numberless narrow views, divided among all sorts of sects. But at least there were plenty of differences and varied points of view, many of them now loosened from anything that may have been restrictive in the medieval discipline. Human reason and imagination, left to themselves, might at least have made as much of Jeanne d'Arc as of John Huss. As a fact, human reason and imagination, left to themselves, made extraordinarily little of her. Humanism and Humanitarianism and, in a general sense, Humanity, did not really rehabilitate Joan until about five hundred years after the Church had done so.

The history of what great men have said about this great woman is a very dismal tale. The greatest man of all, Shakespeare, has an unfortunate pre-eminence by his insular insults in HENRY THE SIXTH. But the thing went on long after Shakespeare; and was far worse in people who had far less excuse than Shakespeare. Voltaire was a Frenchman; he was a great Frenchman; he professed an admiration for many French heroes; he certainly professed to be a reformer and a friend of freedom; he most certainly might have seized on any mediaeval miscarriage of justice that might be turned to anti-clerical account. What Voltaire wrote about St. Joan it will be most decent to pass over in silence. But it is the same all along the line; it is the same far later in rationalistic history than Voltaire. Byron had with all his faults a sensibility to the splendid and heroic, especially in the matter of nations struggling to be free. He was far less insular than any other English poet; he had far more comprehension of France and of the Continent; and he is still comprehended and admired there. He called St. Joan of Arc a fanatical strumpet. That was the general tone of human culture, of history as taught and talked in the age of reason. Mr. Belloc has noted that, so strong was this secular social pressure, that even a Catholic, when he wished to be moderate, like Lingard, was more or less sceptical, not indeed of the morality, but certainly of the miraculous mission of St. Joan. It is true that Schiller was sympathetic, though sentimental—and therefore out of touch. But it was not till nearly the end of the nineteenth century, not fully until the beginning of the twentieth century, that ordinary men of genius awoke to the recognition of one of the most wonderful women of genius in the history of the world. One of the first really popular attempts at a rationalist rehabilitation came, of all people in the world, from Mark Twain. His notion of the Middle Ages was as provincial as the Yankee at the Court of King Arthur; but it is to the credit of this rather crude genius, of the late culture of a new country, that he did catch the flame from the pyre of Rouen, which so many cultivated sceptics had found cold. Then came a patronising pamphlet by Anatole France; which I for one think rather more insulting than the ribald verse of Voltaire. Then came the last great attempt; wrong in many ways in its contention, but conspicuously spirited and sincere—the play of St. Joan. On the whole, nobody can say that humanists and rationalists have been very early in the field. This heroine had to wait about five centuries for Bernard Shaw.

Now, in that comparison, nobody can say that the Church comes off very badly in comparison with the world. The truth is that the ecclesiastical apology to the martyr came so early that everybody had forgotten all about it, long before the rest of the world began to consider the question at all. And though I have taken here the particular case of St. Joan of Arc, I believe that something of the same sort could be traced through a great many other affairs in human history.

It is true of those who gave the Jesuits a bad name and hanged them; and the hanging was not always metaphorical. The simplified version of it is to say that the Jesuits, especially in their capacity of Casuists, suffered almost entirely from being two hundred years before their time. They tried to start in a cautious way what is now surging up on every side of us in a chaotic way; all that is implied in talking about problem novels and problem plays. In other words, they recognised that there really are problems in moral conduct; not problems about whether the moral law should be obeyed, but problems about how in a particular case the moral law really applies. But they were not remembered as pioneers who had begun to ask the questions of Ibsen and Hardy and Shaw. They were remembered only as wicked conspirators who had not always believed in the Divine Right of Kings. They pioneered early enough to be execrated by an earlier generation; but too early to be thanked by a later generation. Protestants have eagerly supported Pascal against them, without taking the trouble to discover that any number of the things that Pascal denounced are things that any modern man would defend. For instance, Pascal blamed the infamous Jesuits for saying that a girl might in some conditions marry against the wish of her parents. The Jesuits would have had all modern novels, let alone problem novels, on their side. But they were too early in the field to have anybody on their side. Moreover, they wished to fit these exceptions into the moral rule; the Moderns who did it two centuries later have produced no rule, but a welter of exceptions.

Here, again, is yet another example that occurs to me at the moment. Many have given long histories of the laborious slowness with which the idea of justice to the aborigines, to Red Indians or such races, has advanced step by step with the progress of modern humanitarian ideas. In such a history Penn, the great Quaker, appears like a primeval founder and father of the republic; and he was undoubtedly very early in the field—in the Puritan field. But Las Casas, the Apostle of the Indians, actually sailed in a ship with Christopher Columbus. It would be difficult to be earlier in the American field than that. He spent his life pleading for the rights of the savages; but he did it at a time when nobody in the north would listen to such a story about a saint of Spain. In this and in many other examples, I believe that the real history of the Catholic pioneer has been the same; to be first and to be forgotten.

PROTESTANTISM: A PROBLEM NOVEL

I HAVE been looking at the little book on Protestantism which Dean Inge has contributed to the sixpenny series of Sir Ernest Benn; and though I suppose it has already been adequately criticised, it may be well to jot down a few notes on it before it is entirely forgotten. The book, which is called "Protestantism, " obviously ought to be called "Catholicism. " What the Dean has to say about any real thing recognisable as Protestantism is extraordinarily patchy, contradictory and inconclusive. It is only what he has to say about Catholicism that is clear, consistent and to the point. It is warmed and quickened by the human and hearty motive of hatred; and it makes everything else in the book look timid and tortuous by comparison. I am not going to annotate the work considered as history. There are some curious, if not conscious, falsifications of fact, especially in the form of suppressions of fact. He begins by interpreting Protestantism as a mere "inwardness and sincerity" in religion; which none of the Protestant reformers would have admitted to be Protestantism, and which any number of Catholic reformers have made the very heart and soul of their reforms inside Catholicism. It might be suggested that self-examination is now more often urged and practised among Catholics than among Protestants. But whether or no the champions of sincerity examine themselves, they might well examine their statements. Some of the statements here might especially be the subject of second thoughts. It is really a startling suppression and falsification to say that Henry the Eighth had only a few household troops; so that his people must have favoured his policy, or they would have risen against it. It seems enough to reply that they did rise against it. And BECAUSE Henry had only a few household troops, he brought in bands of ferocious mercenaries from abroad to put down the religious revolt of his own people. It is an effort of charity to concede even complete candour to the story-teller, who can actually use such an argument, and then keep silent upon such a sequel. Or again, it is outrageously misleading to suggest that the Catholic victims of Tudor and other tyranny were justly executed as traitors and not as martyrs to a religion. Every persecutor alleges social and secular necessity; so did Caiaphas and Annas; so did Nero and Diocletian; from the first the Christians were suppressed as enemies of the Empire; to the last the heretics were handed over to the secular arm with secular justifications. But when, in point of plain fact, a man can be hanged, drawn and quartered merely for saying Mass, or sometimes for helping somebody who has said Mass, it is simply raving nonsense to say that a religion is not being persecuted. To mention only one of many minor falsifications of this kind, it is quite true to say that Milton was in many ways more of a Humanist than a Puritan; but it is quite false to suggest that the Milton family was a typical Puritan family, in its taste for music and letters. The very simple explanation is that the Milton family was largely a Catholic family; and it was the celebrated John who specially separated himself from its creed but retained its culture. Countless other details as definitely false could be quoted; but I am much more interested in the general scope of the work— which allows itself to be so curiously pointless about Protestantism, merely in order to make a point against Catholicism.

Here is the Dean's attempt at a definition. "What is the main function of Protestantism? It is essentially an attempt to check the tendency to corruption and degradation which attacks every institutional religion. " So far, so good. In that case St. Charles Borromeo, for instance, was obviously a leading Protestant. St. Dominic and St. Francis, who purged the congested conventionalism of much of the monasticism around them, were obviously leading Protestants. The Jesuits who sifted legend by the learning of Bollandism, were obviously leading Protestants. But most living Protestant leaders are not leading Protestants. If degradation drags down EVERY institutional religion, it has presumably dragged down Protestant institutional religion. Protestants might possibly appear to purge Protestantism; but so did Catholics appear to purge Catholicism. Plainly this definition is perfectly useless as a DISTINCTION between Protestantism and Catholicism. For it is not a description of any belief or system or body of thought; but simply of a good intention, which all men of all Churches would profess and a few men in some Churches practise—especially in ours. But the Dean not only proves that modern Protestant institutions ought to be corrupt, he says that their primitive founders ought to be repudiated. He distinctly holds that we cannot follow Luther and Calvin.

Very well—let us go on and see whom we are to follow. I will take one typical passage towards the end of the book. The Dean first remarks, "The Roman Church has declared that there can be no reconciliation between Rome and modern Liberalism or Progress. " One would like to see the encyclical or decree in which this declaration was made. Liberalism might mean many things, from the special thing which Newman denounced and defined to the intention of voting at a by-election for Sir John Simon. Progress generally means something which the Pope has never, so far as I know, found it necessary to deny; but which the Dean himself has repeatedly and most furiously denied. He then goes on: "Protestantism is entirely free from this uncompromising preference for the Dark Ages. " "The Dark Ages, " of course, is cant and claptrap; we need take no notice of that. But we may perhaps notice, not without interest and amusement, that about twenty-five lines before, the Dean himself has described the popular Protestantism of America as if it were a barbarism and belated obscurantism. From which one may infer that the Dark Ages are still going on, exactly where there is Protestantism to preserve them. And considering that he says at least five times that the appeal of Protestants to the letter of Scripture is narrow and superstitious, it surely seems a little astonishing that he should sum up by declaring Protestantism, as such, to be "ENTIRELY free" from this sort of darkness. Then, on top of all this welter of wordy contradictions, we have this marvellous and mysterious conclusion: "It is in this direction that Protestants may look for the beginning of what may really be a new Reformation, a resumption of the unfinished work of Sir Thomas More, Giordano Bruno and Erasmus. "

In short, Protestants may look forward to a Reformation modelled on the work of two Catholics and one obscure mystic, who was not a Protestant and of whose tenets they and the world know practically nothing. One hardly knows where to begin, in criticising this very new Reformation, two-thirds of which was apparently started by men of the Old Religion. We might meekly suggest that, if it be regrettable that the work of Sir Thomas More was "unfinished, " some portion of the blame may perhaps attach to the movement that cut off his head. Is it possible, I wonder, that what the Dean really means is that we want a new Reformation to undo all the harm that was done by the old Reformation? In this we certainly have no reason to quarrel with him. We should be delighted also to have a new Reformation, of ourselves as well as of Protestants and other people; though it is only fair to say that Catholics did, within an incredibly short space of time, contrive to make something very like a new Reformation; which is commonly called the Counter-Reformation. St. Vincent de Paul and St. Francis of Sales have at least as good a right to call themselves inheritors of the courtesy and charity of More as has the present Dean of St.

Paul's. But putting that seventeenth century reform on one side, there is surely something rather stupendous about the reform that the Dean proposes for the twentieth century, and the patron saints he selects for it out of the sixteenth century.

For this, it seems, is how we stand. We are not to follow Luther and Calvin. But we are to follow More and Erasmus. And that, if you please, is the true Protestantism and the promise of a second Reformation. We are to copy the views and virtues of the men who found they could remain under the Pope, and especially of one who actually died for the supremacy of the Pope. We are to throw away practically every rag of thought or theory that was held by the people who did not remain under the supremacy of the Pope. And we are to bind up all these views in a little popular pamphlet with an orange cover and call them "Protestantism. " The truth is that Dean Inge had an impossible title and an impossible task. He had to present Protestantism as Progress; when he is far too acute and cultivated a man not to suspect that it was (as it was) a relapse into barbarism and a break away from all that was central in civilisation. Even by the test of the Humanist, it made religion inhuman. Even by the test of the liberal, it substituted literalism for liberalism. Even if the goal had been mere Modernism, it led its followers to it by a long, dreary and straggling detour, a wandering in the wilderness, that did not even discover Modernism till it had first discovered Mormonism. Even if the goal had been logical scepticism, Voltaire could reach it more rapidly from the school of the Jesuits than the poor Protestant provincial brought up among the Jezreelites. Every mental process, even the process of going wrong, is clearer in the Catholic atmosphere. Protestantism has done nothing for Dean Inge, except give him a Deanery which rather hampers his mental activity. It has done nothing for his real talent or scholarship or sense of ideas. It has not in history defended any of the ideas he defends, or helped any of the liberties in which he hopes. But it has done one thing: it has hurt something he hates. It has done some temporary or apparent harm to the heritage of St. Peter. It once made something that looked like a little crack in the wall of Rome. And because of THAT, the Dean can pardon anything to the Protestants—even Protestantism.

For this is the strange passion of his life; and he toils through all these pages of doubts and distinctions only for the moment when he can liberate his soul in one wild roar of monomaniac absurdity: "Let the innocent Dreyfus die in prison; let the Irishman who has committed a treacherous murder be told to leave 'politics' out of his confession; let the lucrative imposture of Lourdes... " That is the way to talk! It is so tiring, pretending to talk sense.

A SIMPLE THOUGHT

MOST men would return to the old ways in faith and morals if they could broaden their minds enough to do so. It is narrowness that chiefly keeps them in the rut of negation. But this enlargement is easily misunderstood, because the mind must be enlarged to see the simple things; or even to see the self-evident things. It needs a sort of stretch of imagination to see the obvious objects against the obvious background; and especially the big objects against the big background. There is always the sort of man who can see nothing but the spot on the carpet, so that he cannot even see the carpet. And that tends to irritation, which he may magnify into rebellion. Then there is the kind of man who can only see the carpet, perhaps because it is a new carpet. That is more human, but it may be tinged with vanity and even vulgarity. There is the man who can only see the carpeted room; and that will tend to cut him off too much from other things, especially the servants' quarters. Finally, there is the man enlarged by imagination, who cannot sit in the carpeted room, or even in the coal-cellar, without seeing all the time the outline of the whole house against its aboriginal background of earth and sky. He, understanding that the roof is raised from the beginning as a shield against sun or snow, and the door against frost or slime, will know better and not worse than the rest the reasons of the rules within. He will know better than the first man that there ought not to be a spot on the carpet. But he will know, unlike the first man, why there is a carpet.

He will regard in the same fashion a speck or spot upon the records of his tradition or his creed. He will not explain it ingeniously; certainly he will not explain it away. On the contrary, he will see it very simply; but he will also see it very largely; and against the background of larger things. He will do what his critics never by any chance do; he will see the obvious thing and ask the obvious question. For the more I read of the modern criticisms of religion, especially of my own religion, the more I am struck by this narrow concentration and this imaginative incapacity to take in the problem as a whole. I have recently been reading a very moderate condemnation of current Catholic practices, coming from America, where the condemnation is often far from moderate. It takes the form, generally speaking, of a swarm of questions, all of which I should be quite willing to answer. Only I am vividly conscious of the big questions that are not asked, rather than of the little questions that are.

And I feel above all, this simple and forgotten fact; that whether certain charges are or are not true of Catholics, they are quite unquestionably true of everybody else. It never occurs to the critic to do anything so simple as to compare what is Catholic with what is Non-Catholic. The one thing that never seems to cross his mind, when he argues about what the Church is like, is the simple question of what the world would be like without it.

That is what I mean by being too narrow to see the house called the church against the background called the cosmos. For instance, the writer of whom I speak indulges in the millionth mechanical repetition of the charge of mechanical repetition. He says that we repeat prayers and other verbal forms without thinking about them. And doubtless there are many sympathisers who will repeat that denunciation after him, without thinking about it at all. But, before we come to explaining the Church's real teaching about such things, or quoting her numberless recommendations of attention and vigilance, or expounding the reason of the reasonable exceptions that she does allow, there is a wide, a simple and a luminous truth about the whole situation which anybody can see if he will walk about with his eyes open. It is the obvious fact that ALL human forms of speech tend to fossilise into formalism; and that the Church stands unique in history not as talking a dead language among everlasting languages; but, on the contrary, as having preserved a living language in a world of dying languages. When the great Greek cry breaks into the Latin of the Mass, as old as Christianity itself, it may surprise some to learn that there are a good many people in church who really do say KYRIE ELEISON and mean exactly what they say. But anyhow, they mean what they say rather more than a man who begins a letter with "Dear Sir" means what he says. "Dear" is emphatically a dead word; in that place it has ceased to have any meaning. It is exactly what the Protestants would allege of Popish rites and forms; it is done rapidly, ritually, and without any memory even of the meaning of the rite. When Mr. Jones the solicitor uses it to Mr. Brown the banker, he does not mean that the banker is dear to him, or that his heart is filled with Christian love, even so much as the heart of some poor ignorant Papist listening to the Mass. Now, life, ordinary, jolly, heathen, human life, is simply chockful of these dead words and meaningless ceremonies. You will not escape from them by escaping from the Church into the world. When the critic in question, or a thousand other critics like him, say that we are only required to make a material or mechanical attendance at Mass, he says something which is NOT true about the ordinary Catholic in his feelings about the Catholic Sacraments. But he says something which IS true about the ordinary official attending official functions, about the ordinary Court levee or Ministerial reception, and about three-quarters of the ordinary society calls and polite visits in the town. This deadening of repeated social action may be a harmless thing; it may be a melancholy thing; it may be a mark of the Fall of Man; it may be anything the critic chooses to think. But those who have made it, hundreds and hundreds of times, a special and concentrated charge against the Church, are men blind to the whole human world they live in and unable to see anything but the thing they traduce.

There are, even in this record, any number of other cases of this queer and uncanny unconsciousness. The writer complains that priests are led blindfold into their calling and do not understand the duties involved in it. That also we seem to have heard before. But we have seldom heard it in so extraordinary a form as in his statement, that a man can be finally committed to the priesthood while he is still "a child. " He would appear to have odd and elastic ideas about the duration of childhood. As Mr. Michael Williams has pointed out in his most thoughtful and illuminating collection of essays, "Catholicism and the Modern Mind, " this is playing about with a matter of plain fact; since a priest is twenty-four at the earliest when he takes his vows. But here again I myself am haunted by this huge and naked and yet neglected comparison between the Church and everything outside the Church. Most critics of Catholicism declare it to be destructive of patriotism; and this critic says something about the disadvantages of the Church being merely "attached to an Italian diocese. " Well, I for one have always been a defender of the cult of patriotism; and nothing that I say here has any connection with what is commonly called pacifism. I think that our friends and brethren fell ten years ago in a just war against the hard heathenism of the north; I think the Prussianism they defeated was frozen with the pride of hell; and for these dead, I think it is well with them; and perhaps better than with us, who live to see how evil Peace can be.

But really—when we come to talk about the Church involving young people in vows! What are we to say to those who would pit patriotism or pagan citizenship against the Church on that issue? They conscript by violence boys of eighteen, they applaud volunteers of sixteen for saying they are eighteen, they throw them by thousands into a huge furnace and torture-chamber, of which their imaginations can have conceived nothing and from which their honour forbids them to escape; they keep them in those horrors year after year without any knowledge even of the possibility of victory; and kill them like flies by the million before they have begun to live. That is what the State does; that is what the World does; that is what their Protestant, practical, sensible, secular society does. And after that they have the astounding impudence to come and complain of us, because in dealing with a small minority of specialists, we allow a man finally to choose a charitable and peaceful life, not only long after he is twenty-one, but when he is well on towards thirty, and after he has had about ten years to think quietly whether he will do it or not!

In short, what I miss in all these things is the obvious thing: the question of how the Church compares with the world outside the Church, or opposed to the Church, or offered as a substitute for the Church. And the fact obviously is that the world will do all that it has ever accused the Church of doing, and do it much worse, and do it on a much larger scale, and do it (which is worst and most important of all) without any standards for a return to sanity or any motives for a movement of repentance. Catholic abuses can be reformed, because there is the admission of a form. Catholic sins can be expiated, because there is a test and a principle of expiation. But where else in the world to-day is any such test or standard found; or anything except a changing mood, which makes patriotism the fashion ten years ago and pacifism the fashion ten years afterwards?

The danger is to-day that men will not sufficiently enlarge their minds to take in the obvious things; and this is one of them. It is that men charge the Roman tradition with being half-heathen and then take refuge from it in a complete heathenism. It is that men complain because Christians have been infected with paganism; and then flee from the plague-spotted to take refuge with the pestilence. There is no single one of these faults alleged against the Catholic institution, which is not far more flagrant and even flamboyant in every other institution. And it is to these other institutions, the State, the School, the modern machinery of taxation and police, to which these people actually look to save them from the superstition of their fathers. That is the contradiction; that is the crashing collision; that is the inevitable intellectual disaster in which they have already involved themselves; and we have only to wait as patiently as we can, to see how long it is before they realise what has happened.

THE CALL TO THE BARBARIANS

A BOOK was sent me the other day by a gentleman who pins his faith to what he calls the Nordic race; and who, indeed, appears to offer that race as a substitute for all religions. Crusaders believed that Jerusalem was not only the Holy City, but the centre of the whole world. Moslems bow their heads towards Mecca and Roman Catholics are notorious for being in secret communication with Rome. I presume that the Holy Place of the Nordic religion must be the North Pole. What form of religious architecture is exhibited in its icebergs, how far its vestments are modified by the white covering of Arctic animals, how the morning and evening service may be adapted to a day and a night each lasting for six months, whether their only vestment is the alb or their only service the angelus of noon, upon all these mysteries I will not speculate. But I can affirm with some confidence that the North Pole is very little troubled by heretical movements or the spread of modern doubt. Anyhow, it would seem that we know next to nothing about this social principle, except that anything is good if it is near enough to the North. And this undoubtedly explains the spiritual leadership of the Eskimo throughout history; and the part played by Spitzbergen as the spiritual arena of modern times. The only thing that puzzles me is that the Englishmen who now call themselves Nordic used to call themselves Teutonic; and very often even Germanic. I cannot think why they altered this so abruptly in the autumn of 1914. Some day, I suppose, when we have diplomatic difficulties with Norway, they will equally abruptly drop the word Nordic. They will hastily substitute some other—I would suggest Borealic. They might be called the Bores, for short.

But I only mention this book because of a passage in it which is rather typical of the tone of a good many other people when they are talking about Catholic history. The writer would substitute one race for all religions; in which he certainly differs from us, who are ready to offer one religion to all races. And even here, perhaps, the comparison is not altogether to his advantage. For anybody who likes can belong to the religion; whereas it is not very clear what is to be done with the people who do not happen to belong to the race. But even among religions he is ready to admit degrees of depravity; he will distinguish between these disgusting institutions; of course, according to their degree of latitude. It is rather unfortunate for him that many Eskimos are Catholics and that most French Protestants live in the south of France; but he proceeds on his general principle clearly enough. He points out, in his pleasant way, why it is exactly that Roman Catholicism is such a degrading superstition. And he adds (which is what interests me at the moment) that this was illustrated in the Dark Ages, which were a nightmare of misery and ignorance. He then admits handsomely that Protestantism is not quite so debased and devilish as Catholicism; and that men of the Protestant nations do exhibit rudimentary traces of the human form. But this, he says, "is not due to their Protestantism, but to their Nordic common sense. " They are more educated, more liberal, more familiar with reason and beauty, because they are what used to be called Teutonic; descended from Vikings and Gothic chiefs rather than from the Tribunes of Florence or the Troubadours of Provence. And in this curious idea I caught a glimpse of something much wider and more interesting; which is another note of the modern ignorance of the Catholic tradition. In speaking of things that people do not know, I have mostly spoken of things that are really within the ring or circle of our own knowledge; things inside the Catholic culture which they miss because they are outside it. But there are some cases in which they themselves are ignorant even of the things outside it. They themselves are ignorant, not only of the centre of civilisation which they slander, but even of the ends of the earth to which they appeal; they not only cannot find Rome on their map, but they do not even know where to look for the North Pole.

Take, for instance, that remark about the Dark Ages and the Nordic common sense. It is tenable and tolerable enough to say that the Dark Ages were a nightmare. But it is nonsense to say that the Nordic element was anything remotely resembling sense. If the Dark Ages were a nightmare, it was very largely because the Nordic nonsense made them an exceedingly Nordic nightmare. It was the period of the barbarian invasions; when piracy was on the high seas and civilisation was in the monasteries. You may not like monasteries, or the sort of civilisation that is preserved by monasteries; but it is quite certain that it was the only sort of civilisation there was. But this is simply one of the things that the Nordic gentleman does not know. He imagines that the Danish pirate was talking about Tariff Reform and Imperial Preference, with scientific statistics from Australia and Alaska, when he was rudely interrupted by a monk named Bede, who had never heard of anything but monkish fables. He supposes that a Viking or a Visigoth was firmly founded on the principles of the Primrose League and the English Speaking Union, and that everything else would have been founded on them if fanatical priests had not rushed in and proclaimed the savage cult called Christianity. He thinks that Penda of Mercia, the last heathen king, was just about to give the whole world the benefits of the British Constitution, not to mention the steam engine and the works of Rudyard Kipling, when his work was blindly ruined by unlettered ruffians with such names as Augustine and Dunstan and Anselm. And that is the little error which invalidates our Nordic friend's importance as a serious historian; that is why we cannot throw ourselves with utter confidence and surrender into the stream of his historical enthusiasm. The difficulty consists in the annoying detail that nothing like what he is thinking about ever happened in the world at all; that the religion of race that he proposes is exactly what he himself calls the Dark Ages. It is what some scientific persons call a purely subjective idea; or in other words, a nightmare. It is very doubtful if there ever was any Nordic race. It is quite certain that there never was any Nordic common sense. The very words "common sense" are a translation from the Latin.

Now that one typical or even trivial case has a larger application. One very common form of Protestant or rationalist ignorance may be called the ignorance of what raw humanity is really like. Such men get into a small social circle, very modern and very narrow, whether it is called the Nordic race or the Rationalist Association. They have a number of ideas, some of them truisms, some of them very untrue, about liberty, about humanity, about the spread of knowledge. The point is that those ideas, whether true or untrue, are the very reverse of universal. They are not the sort of ideas that any large mass of mankind, in any age or country, may be assumed to have. They may in some cases be related to deeper realities; but most men would not even recognise them in the form in which these men present them. There is probably, for instance, a fundamental assumption of human brotherhood that is common to all humanity. But what we call humanitarianism is not common to humanity. There is a certain recognition of reality and unreality which may be called common sense. But the scientific sense of the special value of truth is not generally regarded as common sense. It is silly to pretend that priests specially persecuted a naturalist, when the truth is that all the little boys would have persecuted him in any village in the world, merely because he was a lunatic with a butterfly-net. Public opinion, taken as a whole is much more contemptuous of specialists and seekers after truth than the Church ever was. But these critics never can take public opinion as a whole. There are a great many examples of this truth; one is the case I have given, the absurd notion that a horde of heathen raiders out of the northern seas and forests, in the most ignorant epoch of history, were not likely to be at least as ignorant as anybody else. They were, of course, much more ignorant than anybody with the slightest social connection with the Catholic Church. Other examples may be found in the story of other religions. Great tracts of the globe, covered in theory by the other religions, are often covered in practice merely by certain human habits of fatalism or pessimism or some other human mood. Islam very largely stands for the fatalism. Buddhism very largely stands for the pessimism. Neither of them knows anything of either the Christian or the humanitarian sort of hope. But an even more convincing experience is to go out into the street, or into a tube or a tram, and talk to the actual cabmen, cooks and charwomen cut off from the Creed by the modern chaos. You will find that heathens are not happy, however Nordic. You will soon find that you do not need to go to Arabia for fatalism; or to the Thibetan desert for despair.

ON THE NOVEL WITH A PURPOSE

I SEE that Mr. Patrick Braybrooke and others, writing to the CATHOLIC TIMES, have raised the question of Catholic propaganda in novels written by Catholics. The very phrase, which we are all compelled to use, is awkward and even false. A Catholic putting Catholicism into a novel, or a song, or a sonnet, or anything else, is not being a propagandist; he is simply being a Catholic. Everybody understands this about every other enthusiasm in the world. When we say that a poet's landscape and atmosphere are full of the spirit of England, we do not mean that he is necessarily conducting an Anti-German propaganda during the Great War. We mean that if he is really an English poet, his poetry cannot be anything but English. When we say that songs are full of the spirit of the sea, we do not mean that the poet is recruiting for the Navy or even trying to collect men for the merchant service. We mean that he loves the sea; and for that reason would like other people to love it. Personally, I am all for propaganda; and a great deal of what I write is deliberately propagandist. But even when it is not in the least propagandist, it will probably be full of the implications of my own religion; because that is what is meant by having a religion. So the jokes of a Buddhist, if there were any, would be Buddhist jokes. So the love-songs of a Calvinistic Methodist, should they burst from him, would be Calvinistic Methodist love-songs. Catholics have produced more jokes and love-songs than Calvinists and Buddhists. That is because, saving their holy presence, Calvinists and Buddhists have not got so large or human a religion. But anything they did express would be steeped in any convictions that they do hold; and that is a piece of common sense which would seem to be quite self-evident; yet I foresee a vast amount of difficulty about it in the one isolated case of the Catholic Church.

To begin with, what I have said would be true of any other real religion; but so much of the modern world is full of a religiosity that is rather a sort of unconscious prejudice. Buddhism is a real religion, or at any rate, a very real philosophy. Calvinism was a real religion, with a real theology. But the mind of the modern man is a curious mixture of decayed Calvinism and diluted Buddhism; and he expresses his philosophy without knowing that he holds it. We say what it is natural to us to say; but we know what we are saying; therefore it is assumed that we are saying it for effect. He says what it is natural to him to say; but he does not know what he is saying, still less why he is saying it. So he is not accused of uttering his dogma with the purpose of revealing it to the world; for he has not really revealed it to himself. He is just as partisan; he is just as particularist; he is just as much depending on one doctrinal system as distinct from another. But he has taken it for granted so often that he has forgotten what it is. So his literature does not seem to him partisan, even when it is. But our literature does seem to him propagandist, even when it isn't.

Suppose I write a story, let us hope a short story, say, about a wood that is haunted by evil spirits. Let us give ourselves the pleasure of supposing that at night all the branches have the appearance of being hung with hundreds of corpses, like the orchard of Louis the Eleventh, the spirits of travellers who have hanged themselves when they came to that spot; or anything bright and cheery like that. Suppose I make my hero, Gorlias Fitzgorgon (that noble character) make the sign of the cross as he passes this spot; or the friend who represents wisdom and experience advise him to consult a priest with a view to exorcism. Making the sign of the cross seems to me not only religiously right, but artistically appropriate and psychologically probable. It is what I should do; it is what I conceive that my friend Fitzgorgon would do; it is also aesthetically apt, or, as they say, "in the picture. " I rather fancy it might be effective if the traveller saw with the mystical eye, as he saw the forest of dead men, a sort of shining pattern or silver tangle of crosses hovering in the dark, where so many human fingers had made that sign upon the empty air. But though I am writing what seems to me natural and appropriate and artistic, I know that the moment I have written it, a great roar and bellow will go up with the word "Propaganda" coming from a thousand throats; and that every other critic, even if he is kind enough to commend the story, will certainly add: "But why does Mr. Chesterton drag in his Roman Catholicism? "

Now let us suppose that Mr Chesterton has not this disgusting habit. Let us suppose that I write the same story, or the same sort of story, informed with a philosophy which is familiar and therefore unobserved. Let us suppose that I accept the ready-made assumptions of the hour, without examining them any more than the others do. Suppose I get into the smooth rut of newspaper routine and political catchwords; and make the man in my story act exactly like the man in the average magazine story. I know exactly what the man in the average magazine story would do. I can almost give you his exact words. In that case Fitzgorgon, on first catching a glimpse of the crowds of swaying spectres in the moon, will almost inevitably say: "But this is the twentieth century! "

In itself, of course, the remark is simply meaningless. It is far more meaningless than making the sign of the cross could ever be; for to that even its enemies attach some sort of meaning. But to answer a ghost by saying, "This is the twentieth century, " is in itself quite unmeaning; like seeing somebody commit a murder and then saying, "But this is the second Tuesday in August! " Nevertheless, the magazine writer who for the thousandth time puts these words into the magazine story, has an intention in this illogical phrase. He is really depending upon two dogmas; neither of which he dares to question and neither of which he is able to state. The dogmas are: first, that humanity is perpetually and permanently improving through the process of time; and, second, that improvement consists in a greater and greater indifference or incredulity about the miraculous. Neither of these two statements can be proved. And it goes without saying that the man who uses them cannot prove them, for he cannot even state them. In so far as they are at all in the order of things that can be proved, they are things that can be disproved. For certainly there have been historical periods of relapse and retrogression; and there certainly are highly organised and scientific civilizations very much excited about the super-natural; as people are about Spiritualism to-day. But anyhow, those two dogmas must be accepted on authority as absolutely true before there is any sense whatever in Gorlias Fitzgorgon saying, "But this is the twentieth century. " The phrase depends on the philosophy; and the philosophy is put into the story.

Yet nobody says the magazine story is propagandist. Nobody says it is preaching that philosophy because it contains that phrase. We do not say that the writer has dragged in his progressive party politics. We do not say that he is going out of his way to turn the short story into a novel with a purpose. He does not feel as if he were going out of his way; his way lies straight through the haunted wood, as does the other; and he only makes Gorlias say what seems to him a sensible thing to say; as I make him do what seems to me a sensible thing to do. We are both artists in the same sense; we are both propagandists in the same sense and non-propagandists in the same sense. The only difference is that I can defend my dogma and he cannot even define his.

In other words, this world of to-day does not know that all the novels and newspapers that it reads or writes are in fact full of certain assumptions, that are just as dogmatic as dogmas. With some of those assumptions I agree, such as the ideal of human equality implied in all romantic stories from CINDERELLA to OLIVER TWIST; that the rich are insulting God in despising poverty. With some of them I totally disagree; as in the curious idea of human inequality, which is permitted about races though not about classes. "Nordic" people are so much superior to "Dagoes, " that a score of Spanish desperados armed to the teeth are certain to flee in terror from the fist of any solitary gentleman who has learned all the military and heroic virtues in Wall Street or the Stock Exchange. But the point about these assumptions, true or false, is that they are felt as being assumed, or alluded to, or taken naturally as they come. They are not felt as being preached; and therefore they are not called propaganda. Yet they have in practice all the double character of propaganda; they involve certain views with which everyone does not agree; and they do in fact spread those views by means of fiction and popular literature. What they do not do is to state them clearly so that they can be criticised. I do not blame the writers for putting their philosophy into their stories. I should not blame them even if they used their stories to spread their philosophy. But they do blame us; and the real reason is that they have not yet realised that we have a philosophy at all.

The truth is, I think, that they are caught in a sort of argument in a circle. Their vague philosophy says to them: "All religion is dead; Roman Catholicism is a religious sect which must be particularly dead, since it consists of mere external acts and attitudes, crossings, genuflections and the rest; which these sectarians suppose they have to perform in a particular place at a particular time. " Then some Catholic will write a romance or a tragedy about the love of a man and woman, or the rivalry of two men, or any other general human affair; and they will be astonished to find that he cannot preach these things in an "unsectarian" way. They say, "Why does he drag in his religion? " They mean, "Why does he drag in his religion, which consists entirely of crossings, genuflections and external acts belonging to a particular place and time, when he is talking about the wide world and the beauty of woman and the anger and ambition of man? " In other words, they say, "When we have assumed that his creed is a small and dead thing, how dare he apply it as a universal and living thing? It has no right to be so broad, when we all know it is so narrow. "

I conclude therefore that, while Mr. Braybrooke was quite right in suggesting that a novelist with a creed ought not to be ashamed of having a cause, the more immediate necessity is to find some way of popularising our whole philosophy of life, by putting it more plainly than it can be put in the symbol of a story. The difficulty with a story is in its very simplicity and especially in its swiftness. Men do things and do not define or defend them. Gorlias Fitzgorgon makes the sign of the cross; he does not stop in the middle of the demon wood to explain why it is at once an invocation of the Trinity and a memorial of the Crucifixion. What is wanted is a popular outline of the way in which ordinary affairs are affected by our view of life, and how it is also a view of death, a view of sex, a view of social decencies, and so on. When people understood the light that shines for us upon all these facts, they would no longer be surprised to find it shining in our fictions.

THE REVOLT AGAINST IDEAS

AT the time when the DAILY EXPRESS communiques provided some pretty awful revelations about Mexico, the DAILY EXPRESS correspondence column provided almost equally awful revelations about England. It gave us a glimpse of what monstrous and misshapen things are still living in our midst, veiled in red brick villas or disguised under bowler hats. The awful revelations about England were, of course, mainly psychological. It was not anarchy in the State, which is the failing of the fighting Latin peoples. It was anarchy in the mind, which is the special character of those whom we call, in moments of anger, Anglo-Saxons. A Mexican atheist would be quite capable of cutting the throat of a priest or training a cannon on a nunnery. But he would be quite incapable of arguing, as the English Protestants did in the newspaper, that it was quite right of Calles to persecute this belief on this occasion, because it was quite wrong of Catholics to persecute any belief on any occasion. No anarchist can be as anarchical as all that. Calles might blow up a St. Peter's but he would not blame a Spaniard for having once done what he was praising a Mexican for trying to do. To that extent even Calles is more of a Catholic as well as more of a Latin. He wants to have his own way, and to prevent thousands of people from having their way; but he does not want to have it both ways. That wild sacrament, the miracle of the vanishing and reappearing cake, of the cake that is ever devoured and ever remaining—that miracle belongs to the religion of unreason and only takes place in the chapels of our own free country.

Amid a welter of such words there was a phrase in one of the letters which is of some sociological interest to us. One of these intolerant tolerationists was endeavouring to defend Calles by suggesting that only prejudice can accuse him of anarchical or anti-religious extremes of opinion. It is quite unfair (it was said) to call Calles an atheist or a Bolshevist. Indeed, we may learn from all these letters that Calles is probably a Wesleyan Methodist and regularly attends a chapel in East Croydon. But he is even worse. They appear to regard it as a favour to Calles to pay him the extraordinary compliment of comparing him to the sixteenth century Reformers. The correspondent here in question uses this as an argument against any alleged anarchism in the Mexican—if he is a Mexican. "Calles and his partisans are branded as Atheists and Bolsheviks—Why? Were the English Reformers Bolsheviks? Certainly not. "

Here we are happily all able to agree. With heartfelt unanimity we can repeat, "Certainly not. " The English Reformers were certainly not Bolshevists. None will withhold the handsome admission that the English Reformers were Capitalists. Few people in history have deserved to be described so exactly, so completely, so typically as Capitalists. They were a great many other things besides Capitalists; some of them were cads, some gentlemen, a few honest men, many thieves, a baser sort courtiers, a better sort monomaniacs; but they were all Capitalists and what they created was Capitalism. They all conducted their powerful political operations on a basis of much accumulated capital; but they never, even with their dying eyes, lost the light of hope and expectation; the promise and the vision of more capital.

But what concerns us nowadays is this; that it is their Capitalism that has remained. As a matter of fact, many of them did have other ideals of spiritual simplification which might in some ways be compared to Communism. We should never be likely to call a man like Cranmer or a man like Burleigh a Bolshevist. We could only say, with Hamlet, that we would he were so honest a man. But there were men in that movement, or that muddle, who were as mad and as honest as Bolshevists. There were theoretical, and especially theological enthusiasms which moved specially towards simplicity; like that of the Bolshevists. But the point to fix and rivet is that THOSE theories are dead. There was a logical and even lofty scheme of thought; but it is that which is utterly abandoned by modern thought. There were sincere ideals in some of the early Protestants; but they are not the ideals of any of the modern Protestants. Thus Calvinism was a clear philosophy; which is alone enough to distinguish it from Modern Thought. But in so far as they had an element of Calvinism, their Calvinism is dead. If they had had an element of Communism, as some of them might, that Communism would now be dead. Nothing but their Capitalism is alive.

We must remember that even to talk of the corruption of the monasteries is a compliment to the monasteries. For we do not talk of the corruption of the corrupt. Nobody pretends that the mediaeval institutions began in mere greed and pride. But the modern institutions did. Nobody says that St. Benedict drew up his rule of labour in order to make his monks lazy; but only that they became lazy. Nobody says that the first Franciscans practised poverty to obtain wealth; but only that later fraternities did obtain wealth. But it is quite certain that the Cecils and the Russells and the rest did from the first want to obtain wealth. That which was death to Catholicism was actually the birth of Capitalism. Since then we have had, not the inconsistency that a man who vowed to be poor became rich; but rather a shocking consistency, that the man who vowed to be rich became richer. After that there was no stopping a race of relative ambition; and a belief in bigger and bigger things. It is indeed true that the Reformers were not Communists. It might be aptly retorted that the Religious were Communists. But the more vital point is not Communism, but a certain comparative spirit. The English squire increased and the English yeoman diminished. Both found their pride in private ownership of land. But the pride was more and more in having a great estate, and not in having an estate. So, in his turn, the English shopkeeper ceased to be proud of minding his own business and could only be proud of the number of businesses he could mind. From this has come all the mercantile megalomania to-day; with its universal transformation of Trades into Trusts. It is the natural conclusion of the movement away from the transformation of all Trades into Guilds. But its genesis was the change from an ideal of humility, in which many failed, to an ideal of pride in which (by its nature) only a few can succeed.

In this sense we may agree with the newspaper correspondent; that the Reformers were not Revolutionists. We can reassure that simple gentleman of our full realisation that they were not Bolshevists. We can entirely absolve the Cranmers and the Cromwells of any restless desire to raise the proletariat. We can clear the great names of Burleigh and Bacon of the stain of any dangerous sympathy with the poor. The distinguishing mark of the Reformers was a profound respect for the powers that be, but an even profounder respect for the wealth that was to be; and a really unfathomable reverence for the wealth that was to be their own. Some people like that spirit, and regard it as the soundest foundation of stable government; we need not argue about it here. It is, broadly speaking, what is regarded as respectability by all those who have nothing else to respect. Certainly nobody could confuse it with revolution. But the point of historical importance could be put in another fashion, also more or less favourable to the Reformers. Capitalism was not only solid, it was in a sense candid. It set up a class to be worshipped openly and frankly because of its wealth. That is the point at the moment and the real contrast between this and the older mediaeval order. Such wealth was the abuse of the monks and abbots; it was the use of the merchants and the squires. The avaricious abbot violated his ideals. The avaricious employer had no ideals to violate. For there never has been, properly speaking, such a thing as the ideal good of Capitalism; though there are any number of good men who are Capitalists following other ideals. The Reformation, especially in England, was above all the abandonment of the attempt to rule the world by ideals, or even by ideas. The attempt had undoubtedly failed, in part, because those who were supposed to be the idealists failed to uphold the ideals; and any number of people who were supposed to accept the general idea thwarted the fulfilment of the ideas. But it also fell under the attack of those who hated, not only those ideals, but any ideals. It was the result of the impatient and imperious appetites of humanity, hating to be restrained by bonds; but most of all to be restrained by invisible bonds. For the English Reformers did not really set up an opposite ideal or an alternative set of ideas. As our friend truly said, they were not Bolshevists. They set up certain very formidable things called facts. They set out almost avowedly to rule the realm merely by facts; by the fact that somebody called Russell had two hundred times more money than any of his neighbours; by the fact that somebody called Cecil had obtained the power of having any of his neighbours hanged. Facts are at least solid while they last; but the fatal thing about them is that they do not last. It is only the ideas that last. And to-day a man may be called Russell and have considerably less money than a man who is called Rockefeller; and history may see the amazing spectacle of a man called Cecil largely thrust out of practical politics and called an idealist and a failure.

The same progress of Capitalism that made the squires has destroyed the squires. The same commercial advance that exalted England before Europe has abased England before America. Exactly in so far as we have our affections healthily attached to this adventurous and patriotic England of the last few centuries, we shall see that our affections and attachments are bound to be betrayed. The process called practical, the attempt to rule merely by facts, has in its own nature the essence of all betrayal. We discover that facts, which seem so solid, are of all things the most fluid. As the professors and the prigs say, facts are always evolving; in other words, they are always evading or escaping or running away. Men who bow down to the wealth of a squire, because it enables him to behave like a gentleman, have to go on bowing down to the same wealth in somebody who cannot behave like a gentleman; and eventually perhaps to the same wealth not attached to any recognisable human being at all, but invested in an irresponsible company in a foreign country. Wealth does indeed take to itself wings, and even abide in the uttermost parts of the sea. Wealth becomes formless and almost fabulous; indeed, they were unconscious satirists who talked about "fabulous wealth. " Great financiers buy and sell thousands of things that nobody has ever seen; and which are for all practical purposes imaginary. So ends the adventure of trusting only to facts; it ends in a fairyland of fantastic abstractions.

We must go back to the idea of government by ideas. There is just that grain of truth in the already mentioned fantasy of Communism. But there were many richer, and subtler and better balanced ideas even in the mediaeval make-up of Catholicism. I repeat that this Catholicism was ruined by Catholics as well as Protestants. Mediaeval sins hampered and corrupted mediaeval ideas, before the Reformers decided to throw away all ideas. But that was the right thing to follow, or to try to follow; and there is not and never will be anything else to do except to try again. Many mediaeval men failed in the attempt to live up to those ideals. But many more modern men are more disastrously failing in the attempt to live without them. And through that failure we shall gradually come to understand the real advantages of that ancient scheme which only partly failed; according to which, in theory at least, the man of peace was higher than the man of war, and poverty superior to wealth.

There is one quaint little phrase in Macaulay's essay on Bacon; that great outbreak of the Philistines against the Philosophers. In one small sentence the great Philistine betrays the weakness of his whole argument of utility. Speaking scornfully of the Schoolmen, he says that St. Thomas Aquinas would doubtless (such was his simplicity) have thought it more important to engage in the manufacture of syllogisms than in the manufacture of gunpowder. Not even the Gunpowder Plot could prevent that sturdy Protestant from assuming that gunpowder is always useful. Since his time we have seen a good deal more gunpowder. One does not need to be a pacifist to think that gunpowder need hardly go on being useful on quite such a grand scale. And a great part of the world has now reached a mood of reaction, in which it is disposed to cry out, "If there are any syllogisms that will save us from all this gunpowder, for God's sake let us listen to them. " Even logic they are prepared, in their despair, to accept. They will not only listen to religion, they will even perhaps listen to reason, if it will promise them a little peace.

THE FEASTS AND THE ASCETIC

I WAS reflecting in the course of the recent feast of Christmas (which, like other feasts, is preceded by a fast) that the combination is still a puzzle to many. The Modernist, or man who boasts of being modern, is generally rather like a man who overeats himself so much on Christmas Eve that he has no appetite on Christmas Day. It is called being In Advance of the Times; and is incumbent upon all who are progressive, prophetic, futuristic and generally looking towards what Mr. Belloc calls the Great Rosy Dawn: a dawn which generally looks a good deal rosier the night before than it does the morning after.

To many people, however, who are not offensively in advance of the times the combination of these ideas does seem to be a sort of contradiction or confusion. But in real fact it is not only not so confused, but even not so complicated. The great temptation of the Catholic in the modern world is the temptation to intellectual pride. It is so obvious that most his critics are talking without in the least knowing what they are talking about, that he is sometimes a little provoked towards the very un-Christian logic of answering a fool according to his folly. He is a little bit disposed to luxuriate in secret, as it were over the much greater subtlety and richness of the philosophy he inherits; and only answer a bewildered barbarian so as to bewilder him still more. He is tempted to ironical agreements or even to disguising himself as a dunce. Men who have an elaborate philosophical defence of their views sometimes take pleasure in boasting of their almost babyish credulity. Having reached their own goal through labyrinths of logic, they will point the stranger only to the very shortest short cut of authority; merely in order to shock the simpleton with simplicity. Or, as in the present case, they will find a grim amusement in presenting the separate parts of the scheme as if they were really separate; and leave the outsider to make what he can of them. So when somebody says that a fast is the opposite to a feast, and yet both seem to be sacred to us, some of us will always be moved merely to say, "Yes, " and relapse into an objectionable grin. When the anxious ethical enquirer says, "Christmas is devoted to merry-making, to eating meat and drinking wine, and yet you encourage this pagan and materialistic enjoyment, " you or I will be tempted to say, "Quite right, my boy, " and leave it at that. When he then says, looking even more worried, "Yet you admire men for fasting in caves and deserts and denying themselves ordinary pleasures; you are clearly committed, like the Buddhists, to the opposite or ascetic principle, " we shall be similarly inspired to say, "Quite correct, old bean, " or "Got it first time, old top, " and merely propose an adjournment for convivial refreshment.

Nevertheless, it is a temptation to be resisted. Not only is it obviously our duty to explain to the other people that what seems to them contradictory is really complementary, but we are not altogether justified in any such tone of superiority. We are not right in making our geniality an expression of our despair. We are not entitled to despair of explaining the truth; nor is it really so horribly difficult to explain. The real difficulty is not so much that the critic is crude as that we ourselves are not always clear, even in our own minds, far less in our public expositions. It is not so much that they are not subtle enough to understand it, as that they and we and everybody else are not simple enough to understand it. Those two things are obviously part of one thing, if we are straightforward enough to look at the thing; and to see it simply as it is. I suggested recently that people would see the Christian story if it could only be told as a heathen story. The Faith is simply the story of a God who died for men. But, queerly enough, if we were even to print the words without a capital G, as if it were the cult of some new and nameless tribe, many would realise the idea for the first time. Many would feel the thrill of a new fear and sympathy if we simply wrote, "the story of a god who died for men. " People would sit up suddenly and say what a beautiful and touching pagan religion that must be.

Let us suppose, for the sake of argument, that the Church is out of the question; that we have nothing but the earth and the children of man pottering about on it, with their normal mortal tales and traditions. Then suppose there appears on this earth a prodigy, a portent, or what is alleged to be a portent. In some way heaven has rent the veil or the gods have given some new marvel to mankind. Suppose, for instance, it is a fountain of magic water, said to be flowing at the top of a mountain. It blesses like holy water; it heals diseases; it inspires more than wine, or those who drink of it never thirst again. Well, this story may be true or false; but among those who spread it as true, it is perfectly obvious that the story will produce a number of other stories. It is equally obvious that those stories will be of two kinds. The first sort will say: "When the water was brought down to the valley there was dancing in all the villages; the young men and maidens rejoiced with music and laughter. A surly husband and wife were sprinkled with the holy water and reconciled, so that their house was full of happy children. A cripple was sprinkled and he went capering about gaily like an acrobat. The gardens were watered and became gay with flowers, " and so on. It is quite equally obvious that there will be another sort of story from exactly the same source, told with exactly the same motive. "A man limped a hundred miles, till he was quite lame, to find the sacred fountain. Men lay broken and bleeding among the rocks on the mountainside in their efforts to climb after it. A man sold all his lands and the rivers running through them for one drop of the water. A man refused to turn back from it, when confronted with brigands, but was tortured and died calling for it, " and so on. There is nothing in the least inconsistent between these two types of legend. They are exactly what would naturally be expected, given the original legend of the miraculous fountain. Anyone who can really look at them simply, can see that they are both equally simple. But we in our time have confused ourselves with long words for unreal distinctions; and talking incessantly about optimism and pessimism, about asceticism and hedonism, about what we call Paganism and what we think about Buddhism, till we cannot understand a plain tale when it is told. The Pagan would have understood it much better.

This very simple truth explains another fact that I have heard the learned insist on with some excitement: the emphasis and repetition touching the ascetic side of religion. It is exactly what would happen with any human story, even if it were a heathen story. We remark upon the case of the man who starves to get the water more than on the case of the man who is merely glad to get the water. We remark upon it more because it is more remarkable. Any human tradition would make more of the heroes who suffered for something than of the human beings who simply benefited by it. But that does not alter the fact that there are more human beings than heroes; and that this great majority of human beings has benefited by it. It is natural that men should marvel more at the man who deliberately lames himself than at the man who dances when he is no longer lame. But that does not alter the fact that the countries where that legend prevails are, in fact, full of dancing. I have here only suggested how very simple, after all, is the contradiction between austerity and jollity which puzzles our critics so much. There is a higher application of it to ascetics, which I may consider on another occasion. Here I will only hint at it by saying: "The more a man could LIVE only on the water, the more he would prove it to be the water of life. "

WHO ARE THE CONSPIRATORS?

I CAME across, more or less indirectly, the other day, a lady of educated and even elegant pretensions, of the sort whom her foes would call luxurious and her friends cultured, who happened to mention a certain small West Country town, and added with a sort of hiss that it contained "a nest of Roman Catholics. " This apparently referred to a family with which I happen to be acquainted. The lady then said, her voice changing to a deep note of doom, "God alone knows what is said and done behind those closed doors. "

On hearing this stimulating speculation, my mind went back to what I remembered of the household in question, which was largely concerned with macaroons, and a little girl who rightly persuaded herself that I could eat an almost unlimited number of them. But when I contrasted that memory with that vision it was brought suddenly and stunningly to my mind what a vast abyss still yawns between us and many of our countrymen, and what extraordinary ideas are still entertained about us, by people who walk about the world without keepers or strait-waistcoats and are apparently, on all other subjects, sane. It is doubtless true, and theologically sound, to say that God alone knows what goes on in Catholic homes; as it is to say that God alone knows what goes on in Protestant heads. I do not know why a Catholic's doors should be any more closed than anybody else's doors; the habit is not unusual in persons of all philosophical beliefs when retiring for the night; and on other occasions depends on the weather and the individual taste. But even those who would find it difficult to believe that an ordinary Catholic is so eccentric as to bolt and padlock himself in the drawing-room or the smoking-room, whenever he strolls into those apartments, do really have a haunting idea that it is more conceivable of a Catholic than of a Calvinistic Methodist or a Plymouth Brother. There does remain the stale savour of a sort of sensational romance about us; as if we were all foreign counts and conspirators. And the really interesting fact is that this absurd melodrama can be found among educated people; though now rather in an educated individual than in an educated class. The world still pays us this wild and imaginative compliment of imagining that we are much less ordinary than we really are. The argument, of course, is the one with which we are wearily familiar in twenty other aspects; the argument that because the evidence against us cannot be produced, it must have been concealed. It is obvious that Roman Catholics do not generally shout to each other the arrangements of a St. Bartholomew Massacre across the public streets; and the only deduction any reasonable man can draw is that they do it behind closed doors. It is but seldom that the project of burning down London is proclaimed in large letters on the posters of the UNIVERSE; so what possible deduction can there be, except that the signals are given at the private tea-table by means of a symbolical alphabet of macaroons? It would be an exaggeration to say that it is my daily habit to leap upon aged Jews in Fleet Street and tear out their teeth; so, given my admitted monomania on the subject, it only remains to suppose that my private house is fitted up like a torture chamber for this mode of mediaeval dentistry. Catholic crimes are not plotted in public, so it stands to reason that they must be plotted in private. There is indeed a third remote and theoretical alternative; that they are not plotted anywhere; but it is unreasonable to expect our fellow-countrymen to suggest anything so fanciful as that.

Now this mysterious delusion, still far commoner than many suppose even in England, and covering whole interior spaces of America, happens to be another illustration of what I have been suggesting in an earlier essay; the fact that those who are always digging and prying for secret things about us, have never even glanced at the most self-evident things about themselves. We have only to ask ourselves, with a sort of shudder, what would have been said if we really had confessed to conspiracy as shamelessly as half our accusers have confessed to it themselves. What in the world would be said, either in America or in Europe, if we really had behaved like a secret society, in places where the groups of our enemies cannot even deny that they are secret societies? What in the world would happen if a Catholic Congress at Glasgow or Leeds really consisted entirely of hooded and white-robed delegates, all with their faces covered and their names unknown, looking out of slits in their ghastly masks of white? Yet this was, until just lately, the rigid routine of the great American organisation to destroy Catholicism; an organisation which recently threatened to seize all government in America. What would have been said, if there really was a definite, recognised, but entirely unknown thing, called the Secret of the Catholics; as there has been for long past a recognised but unknown reality called the Secret of the Freemasons? I dare say a great deal involved in such things is mere harmless foolery. But if we had done such things, would our critics have said it was harmless foolery? Suppose we had started to spread the propaganda of the

Faith by means of a movement called "Know Nothing, " because we were in the habit of always shaking our heads and shrugging our shoulders and swearing that we knew nothing of the Faith we meant to spread. Suppose our veneration for the dignity of St. Peter were wholly and solely a veneration for the denial of St. Peter; and we used it as a sort of motto or password to swear that we knew not Christ. Yet that was admittedly the policy of a whole political movement in America, which aimed at destroying the citizenship of Catholics. Suppose that the Mafia and all the murderous secret associations of the Continent had been notoriously working on the Catholic side, instead of the other side. Should we ever have heard the last of it? Would not the world have rung with indignant denunciation of a disgrace clinging to all our conduct, and a treason that must never be forgot? Yet these things are done constantly, and at regular intervals, and right down to the present day, by the Anti-Catholic parties; and it is never thought necessary to recall them, or say a word of apology for them, in the writings of any Anti-Catholic partisan. It would be just our Jesuitical way to dare to look over hedges, when everybody else is only stealing horses.

In short, what I recently said of bigotry is even more true of secrecy. In so far as there is something merely antiquated about a certain type of doctrinal narrowness, it is much more characteristic of Dayton, Tennessee, than of Louvain or Rome. And in the same way, in so far as there is something antiquated about all these antics in masks and cloaks, it has been much more characteristic of the Ku Klux Klan than of the Jesuits. Indeed, this sort of Protestant is a figure of old-fashioned melodrama in a double sense and in a double aspect. He is antiquated in the plots he attributes to us and in the plots that he practises himself.

As regards the latter, it is probable that the whole world will discover this fact a long time before he does. The anti-clerical will go on playing solemnly the pranks of Cagliostro, like a medium still blindfolded in broad daylight; and will open his mouth in mysteries long after everybody in the world is completely illuminated about the illuminati. And though the almost half-witted humour of the American society, which seemed to consist entirely of beginning as many words as possible with KL, has been rather abruptly toned down by a reaction of relative sanity, I have no doubt that there is still many a noble Nordic fellow going about hugging himself over the happy secret that he is a Kleagle or a Klemperor, long after everybody has ceased to klare a klam whether he is or not. On the political side the power of these conspiracies has been practically broken in both Continents; in Italy by the Fascists and in America by a rally of reasonable and public-spirited governors of both political parties. But the point of historical interest remains: that it was the very people who accused us of mummery and mystery who surrounded all their secularising activities with far more fantastic mysteries and mummeries; that they had not even the manhood to fight an ancient ritual with the appearance of republican simplicity, but boasted of hiding everything in a sort of comic complexity; even when there was nothing to hide. By this time such movements as the Ku Klux Klan have very little left which can be hidden or which is worth hiding; and it is therefore probable that our romantic curiosity about them will be considerably colder than their undying romantic curiosity about us. The Protestant lady will continue to resent the fact that God does not share with her his knowledge of the terrible significance of tea and macaroons in the Catholic home. But we shall probably in the future feel a fainter and fainter interest in whatever it is that Kleagues do behind closed— or perhaps I should say Klosed Doors.

THE HAT AND THE HALO

PERHAPS it is a little ungenerous to refer again to the fiasco of the unfortunate Bishop of Birmingham, when he made an exhibition of himself on the subject of St. Francis. That he should be unable to restrain himself from attacking one whom so many free-thinkers have loved and reverenced is interesting as showing how far sectarians can go. But the tone of the attack raises a question more interesting than the personal one. It may be called broadly the question of Sentiment; but it involves the whole question of what things in life are deep and what things shallow; what is central and what is merely external. It is needless to say that people like the Bishop invariably and instinctively get them the wrong way round.

For instance, he said something to the effect that people are now seeing St. Francis in a halo of false sentiment, or through a haze of false sentiment. I am not sure which he said and I doubt whether he knew which he meant. If the Bishop had a halo it would probably be rather like a haze. But anyhow he implied that the hero-worship of St. Francis was a sort of external and extraneous thing, a dazzling distraction or a distorting medium, something added to his figure afterwards; whereas the facts about the real St. Francis were quite different and decidedly repulsive to a refined person. Well, the poor Bishop got all his facts about St. Francis quite wrong; and his claim to talk about the REAL St. Francis, even in an ordinary historical sense, was pretty rapidly shown up. But there was something behind it which interests me much more. It is the curious trick of turning everything inside out; so that the really central things become external and the merely external things central. The inmost soul of St. Francis is a haze of false sentiment; but the accidents of his historical setting, as viewed by people without any historical sense, are a sort of dreadful secret of his soul.

According to this sort of criticism, St. Francis had a great soul; which was merely a cloak for a miserable body. It is sentimental to consider what he felt like. But it is realistic to consider what he looked like. Or rather it is realistic to consider what he would have looked like to the best-dressed people in Birmingham who never saw him, or the fashionable tailor in Bond Street who never had the opportunity of making him a suit of clothes. The critic tells us what some hypothetical suburban snob of the twentieth century would have thought of the Saint he never saw; and THAT is the real truth about the Saint. We can tell him what the Saint would have thought of the suburban snob (and his thoughts would have been full of the simple and spontaneous tenderness which he showed to all small and helpless creatures) but that is only sentiment about St. Francis. What St Francis himself felt about all other creatures is only a misleading and artificial addition to his character. But what some of the most limited and least imaginative of those creatures might possibly think about him, or rather about his clothes or his meals—that alone is reality.

When the admirers of St. Francis, who number myriads of Protestants and Agnostics as well as Catholics, say that they admire that great man, they mean that they admire his mind, his affections, his tastes, his point of view. They mean that, like any other poet, he puts them in a position to view the world in a certain way; and that life looked at from his mental standpoint is more inspiring or intelligible. But when the Bishop tells them that they do not know the facts about St. Francis, he does not mean that St. Francis had some other mind or some other standpoint. He means that St. Francis did not have hot and cold water laid on in the bathroom, did not put on a clean collar every morning, did not send a sufficient number of shirts to the Birmingham Imperial Laundry every week, did not have black mud smeared on his boots or white mud to stiffen his shirt front, and all the rest of it. And THAT is what he calls the truth about St. Francis! Everything else, including everything that St. Francis did do, is a haze of sentiment.

That is the deeper problem of which this foolish affair happens to be an illustration. How are we to make these superficial people understand that we are not being sentimental about St. Francis, that we are not presenting an elegant and poetical picture of St. Francis; that we are not presenting irresponsible emotional ravings about St. Francis; that we are simply presenting St. Francis? We are presenting a remarkable mind; just as Plato presented a remarkable mind, whether it was his own or somebody else's. We think no more of Bishop Barnes and his nonsense than a Platonist would think about some joke in Aristophanes about Socrates catching fleas. There may have been people who saw that mind through a haze of false sentiment; there were people who saw it through a haze of exaggerated enthusiasm; like those heretics who made St. Francis greater than Christ and the founder of a new dispensation. But even those fanatics were more like philosophers than a gentleman who is content to say either of a true saint or a false god, that his taste in linen and steam laundries was "not ours. " In short, the true situation is simple and obvious enough. It is we who are thinking about the real Francis Bernadone, even the realistic Francis Bernadone, the actual man whose mind and mood we admire. It is the critic who is thinking of the unreal Francis, a fantastic phantom produced by looking at him in a Bond Street looking-glass or comparing him with the fashion-plates of 1926. If it is well for a man to be happy, to have the way of welcoming the thing that happens and the next man that comes along, then St. Francis was happy; happier than most modern men. If it be good that a man should be sympathetic, should include a large number of things in his imaginative sympathy, should have a hospitality of the heart for strange things and strange people, then St. Francis was sympathetic; more sympathetic than most modern men. If it be good that a man should be original, should add something creative and not merely customary or conventional, should do what he thinks right in his own way and without fear of worldly consequences in ruin or starvation, then St. Francis was original; more original than most modern men. All these are tests at once personal and permanent; they deal with the very essence of the ego or individual and they are not affected by changes in external fashion. To say that these things are mere sentiment is to say that the inmost sense of the inmost self is mere sentiment. And yet how are we to stop superficial people from calling it mere sentiment? How are we to make them realise that it is not we who have a sentimental attachment to a mediaeval friar, but they who have an entirely sentimental attachment to certain modern conventions?

Such critics have never really thought of asking what they mean by "sentiment, " still less what they mean by "false sentiment. " "False" is simply a conventional term of abuse to be applied to "sentiment"; and "sentiment" is simply a conventional term of abuse to be applied to Catholicism. But it is very much more applicable nowadays to Protestantism. It is especially applicable to Bishop Barnes's own rather nebulous type of Protestantism. Men of his school always complain of our thinking too much of theology, just as they complained a few centuries before of our thinking too little of theology. But theology is only the element of reason in religion; the reason that prevents it from being a mere emotion. There are a good many broad-minded persons for whom it is only an emotion; and it would hardly be unfair to say it is only a sentiment. And we have not to look far for them in cases like these.

If a school of critics were found prepared to pay divine honours to a certain person while doubting whether he was divine, men who took off their hats in his churches while denying that he was present on his altars, who hinted that he was only a religious teacher and then hinted again that he must be served as if he were the only teacher of religion; who are always ready to treat him as a fallible individual in relation to his rivals, and then to invoke him as an infallible authority against his followers, who dismiss every text they choose to think dogmatic and then gush over every text they choose to think amiable, who heckle him with Higher Criticism about three-quarters of what he said and then grovel before a mawkish and unmanly ideal made by misunderstanding the little which is left—if there were a school of critics in THIS relation to a historical character, we might very well admit that they were not getting to grips with it, but surrounding it with "a halo of false sentiment. "

That is the vital distinction. At least we do not admit sentiment as a substitute for statement; still less as a contradiction of something that we state. There may be devotional expressions that are emotional, and even extravagantly emotional; but they do not actually distort any definition that is purely intellectual. But in the case of our critics, the confusion is in the intellect. We do not claim that all our pictorial or poetical expressions are adequate; but the fault is in the execution not in the conception. And there is a conception which is not a confusion. We do not say that every pink and blue doll from an Art Repository is a satisfactory symbol of the Mother of God. But we do say that it is less of a contradiction than exists in a person who says there is no Original Sin in anybody, and then calls it Mariolatry to say there was no Original Sin in Mary. We do not profess to admire the little varnished pictures of waxen angels or wooden children around the Communion Table. But we do most strongly profess and proclaim that they are less of a blot on the intellectual landscape than a bishop who suggests that the Host may actually be the divine Presence, but that High Church curates will do his lordship a personal favour if they take no notice of it. We are under no illusions about the literary quality of a large number of hymns in our hymn-books, or any other hymn-books. But we modestly submit that though they are doggerel they are not nonsense; and that saying that we can assert a personal God, a personal immortality, a personal divine love that extends to the least and worst, and do all this without holding "a Creed, " IS nonsense. We know that the nearest sane agnostic or atheist would agree that it is nonsense. Devotional art and literature are often out of balance or broken in expression;

sometimes because the emotion is too real and too strong for the reason, the same thing which makes the love-letters of the wisest men like the letters of lunatics; sometimes from a real deficiency in the individual power of reason; but never from a theoretical repudiation of reason, like that of the Pragmatists and about three-quarters of the Modernists. And in the same way it is the very reverse of the truth to say that a mere emotional distortion of the facts has drawn the modern mind towards St. Francis. It is, on the contrary, emphatically an attraction of mind to mind; and the more purely mental the process, the less it will be interrupted by ignorant irritation against the strangeness of Italian manners or mediaeval conditions. And in this case there is no international problem. Thousands of Englishmen who know nothing but England glow with love and understanding of St. Francis. We may well feel an unaffected pity for the one unlucky Englishman who cannot understand.

ON TWO ALLEGORIES

PERHAPS it is only fair that the modern iconoclasm should be applied also to the ancient iconoclasts; and especially to the great Puritans, those idol-breakers who have long been idols. Mr. Belloc was recently tapping the Parliamentary statue of Cromwell with a highly scientific hammer; and Mr. Noyes has suddenly assailed the image of Bunyan with something more like a sledge-hammer. In the latter case I confess to thinking the reaction excessive; I should say nothing worse of Bunyan than of many old writers; that he is best known by his best passages, and that many, who fondly believe they have read him, would be mildly surprised at some of his worst passages. But that is not peculiar to Bunyan; and I for one should be content with saying what I said some years ago. A fair and balanced view of the culture and creeds involved can best be reached by comparing the Pilgrimage of Christian with the Pilgrimage of Piers Plowman. The Puritan allegory is much neater (even if it be not always neat) than the rather bewildering mediaeval medley. The Puritan allegory is more national, in the sense that the language and style have obviously become clearer and more fixed. But the Puritan allegory is certainly much narrower than the mediaeval allegory. Piers Plowman deals with the death or resurrection of a whole human society, where men are members of each other. In the later work schism has "isolated the soul"; and it is certainly mere individualism, when it is not mere terrorism. But I will only say now what I said then; I do not want to damage the statue of John Bunyan at Bedford, where it stands facing (symbolically in more ways than one) the site of his own prison. But I do wish there were a statue of John Langland, uplifted on a natural height into a more native air, and looking across all England from the Malvern hills.

But there is one intellectual side issue of the debate that does interest me very much. Mr. James Douglas, who once presented himself to me as a representative of Protestant truth, and who is certainly a representative of Protestant tradition, answered Mr. Alfred Noyes in terms very typical of the present state of that tradition. He said that we should salute Bunyan's living literary genius, and not bother our heads about Bunyan's obsolete theology. Then he added the comparison which seems to me so thought-provoking: that this is after all what we do, when we admire Dante's genius and not HIS obsolete theology. Now there is a distinction to be made here; if the whole modern mind is to realize at all where it stands. If I say that

Bunyan's theology IS obsolete, but Dante's theology is NOT obsolete—then I know the features of my friend Mr. Douglas will be wreathed in a refined smile of superiority and scorn. He will say that I am a Papist and therefore of course I think the Papist dogmatism living. But the point is that he is a Protestant and he thinks the Protestant dogmatism dead. I do at least defend the Catholic theory because it can be defended. The Puritans would presumably be defending the Puritan theory— if it could be defended. The point is that it is dead for them as much as for us. It is not merely that Mr. Noyes demands the disappearance of a disfigurement; it is that Mr. Douglas says it cannot be a disfigurement because it has already disappeared. Now the Thomist philosophy, on which Dante based his poetry has not disappeared. It is not a question of faith but of fact; anybody who knows Paris or Oxford, or the worlds where such things are discussed, will tell you that it has not disappeared. All sorts of people, including those who do not believe in it, refer to it and argue against it on equal terms.

I do not believe, for a fact, that modern men so discuss the seventeenth century sectarianism. Had I the privilege of passing a few days with Mr. Douglas and his young lions of the DAILY EXPRESS, I doubt not that we should discuss and differ about many things. But I do rather doubt whether Mr. Douglas would every now and again cry out, as with a crow of pure delight "Oh, I must read you this charming little bit from Calvin. " I do rather doubt whether his young journalists are joyously capping each other's quotations from Toplady's sermons on Calvinism. But eager young men do still quote Aquinas, just as they still quote Aristotle. I have heard them at it. And certain ideas are flying about, even in the original prose of St. Thomas, as well as in the poetry of Dante—or, for that matter, of Donne.

The case of Bunyan is really the opposite of the case of Dante. In Dante the abstract theory still illuminates the poetry; the ideas enlighten even where the images are dark. In Bunyan it is the human facts and figures that are bright; while the spiritual background is not only dark in spirit, but blackened by time and change. Of course it is true enough that in Dante the mere images are immensely imaginative. It is also true that in one sense some of them are obsolete; in the sense that the incidents are obsolete and the personal judgment merely personal. Nobody will ever forget how there came through the infernal twilight the figure of that insolent troubadour, carrying his own head aloft in his hand like a lantern to light his

way. Everybody knows that such an image is poetically true to
certain terrible truths about the unnatural violence of intellectual
pride. But as to whether anybody has any business to say that
Bertrand de Born is damned, the obvious answer is No. Dante knew
no more about it than I do: only he cared more about it; and his
personal quarrel is an obsolete quarrel. But that sort of thing is not
Dante's theology, let alone Catholic theology.

In a word; so far from his theology being obsolete, it would be much
truer to say that everything is obsolete except his theology. That he
did not happen to like a particular Southern gentleman is obsolete;
but that was at most a private fancy, in demonology rather than
theology. We come to theology when we come to theism. And if
anybody will read the passage in which Dante grapples with the
gigantic problem of describing the Beatific Vision, he will find it is
uplifted into another world of ideas from the successful entry to the
Golden City at the end of the Pilgrim's Progress. It is a Thought;
which a thinker, especially a genuine freethinker, is always free to go
on thinking. The images of Dante are not to be worshipped, any
more than any other images. But there is an idea behind all images;
and it is before that, in the last lines of the Paradiso, that the spirit of
the poet seems first to soar like an eagle and then to fall like a stone.

There is nothing in this comparison that reflects on the genius and
genuineness of Bunyan in his own line or class; but it does serve to
put him in his own class. I think there was something to be said for
the vigorous denunciation of Mr. Noyes; but no such denunciation is
involved in this distinction. On the contrary, it would be easy to
draw the same distinction between two men both at the very top of
all literary achievement. It would be true to say, I think, that those
who most enjoy reading Homer care more about an eternal
humanity than an ephemeral mythology. The reader of Homer cares
more about men than about gods. So, as far as one can guess, does
Homer. It is true that if those curious and capricious Olympians did
between them make up a religion, it is now a dead religion. It is the
human Hector who so died that he will never die. But we should
remonstrate with a critic who, after successfully proving this about
Homer, should go on to prove it about Plato. We should protest if he
said that the only interest of the Platonic Dialogues to-day is in their
playful asides and very lively local colour, in the gay and graceful
picture of Greek life; but that nobody troubles nowadays about the
obsolete philosophy of Plato. We should point out that there is no
truth in the comparison; and that if anything the case is all the other

way. Plato's philosophy will be important as long as there is philosophy; and Dante's religion will be important as long as there is religion. Above all it will be important as long as there is that lucid and serene sort of religion that is most in touch with philosophy. Nobody will say that the theology of the Baptist tinker is in that sense serene or even lucid; on many points it necessarily remains obscure. The reason is that such religion does not do what philosophy does; it does not begin at the beginning. In the matter of mere chronological order, it is true that the pilgrimage of Dante and that of Bunyan both end in the Celestial City. But it is in a very different sense that the pilgrimage of Bunyan begins in the City of Destruction. The mind of Dante, like that of his master St. Thomas, really begins as well as ends in the City of Creation. It begins as well as ends in the burning focus in which all things began. He sees his series from the right end, though he then begins it at the wrong end. But it is the whole point of a personal work like THE PILGRIM'S PROGRESS that it does begin with a man's own private sins and private panic about them. This intense individualism gives it great force; but it cannot in the nature of things give it great breadth and range. Heaven is haven; but the wanderer has not many other thoughts about it except that it is haven. It is typical of the two methods, each of them very real in its way, that Dante could write a whole volume, one-third of his gigantic epic, describing the things of Heaven; whereas in the case of Bunyan, as the gates of Heaven open the book itself closes.

I think it worth while to write this note on the critical remark of Mr. James Douglas, because it is a remark that would be made as readily by many other intelligent men to-day. But it is founded on a fallacy; on the idea that the choice between living philosophies and dead philosophies is the same as the choice between old philosophies and new. It is not true of Plato and it is not true of Dante; and, apart from whatever is our own philosophy, we should realise that some of the most ancient are the most alive.

THE PROTESTANT SUPERSTITIONS

THAT delightful guessing game, which has long caused innocent merriment in so many Catholic families, the game of guessing at exactly which line of an article say on Landscape or Latin Elegiacs, we shall find the Dean of St. Paul's introducing the Antidote to Antichrist; or the Popish Plot Revealed—that most familiar of our Catholic parlour games happened to be entertaining me some time ago, as a sort of substitute for a crossword puzzle, when I found I had hit on a very lucky example. I wrote above about "Catholic families, " and had almost, by force of associations written "Catholic firesides. " And I imagine that the Dean really does think that even in this weather we keep the home-fires burning, like the fire of Vesta, in permanent expectation of relighting the fires of Smithfield. Anyhow, this sort of guessing game or crossword puzzle is seldom disappointing. The Dean must by this time have tried quite a hundred ways of leading up to his beloved topic; and even concealing it, like a masked battery, until he can let loose the cannonade in a perfect tornado of temper. Then the crossword puzzle is no longer a puzzle, though the crosswords are apparent and appropriate enough; especially those devoted to the great historical process of crossing out the Cross.

In the case of this particular article, it was only towards the end of it that the real subject was allowed to leap out from an ambush upon the reader. I think it was a general article on Superstition; and, being a journalistic article of the modern type, it was of course devoted to discussing superstition without defining superstition. In an article of that enlightened sort, it seemed enough for the writer to suggest that superstition is anything that he does not happen to like. Some of the things are also things that I do not happen to like. But such a writer is not reasonable even when he is right. A man ought to have some more philosophical objection to stories of ill luck than merely calling them credulity; as certainly as a man ought to have some more philosophical objection to Mass than to call it Magic. It is hardly a final refutation of Spiritualists to prove that they believe in Spirits; any more than a refutation of Deists to prove that they believe in Deity. Creed and credence and credulity are words of the same origin and can be juggled backwards and forwards to any extent. But when a man assumes the absurdity of anything that anybody else believes, we wish first to know what he believes; on what principle he believes; and, above all, upon what principle he disbelieves. There is no trace of anything so rational in the Dean's piece of metaphysical journalism. If he had stopped to define his terms, or in other words to tell us what he was talking about, such an abstract analysis would of course have filled up some space in the article. There might have been no room for the Alarum Against the Pope.

The Dean of St. Paul's got to business, in a paragraph in the second half of his article, in which he unveiled to his readers all the horrors of a quotation from Newman; a very shocking and shameful passage in which the degraded apostate says that he is happy in his religion, and in being surrounded by the things of his religion; that he likes to have objects that have been blessed by the holy and beloved, that there is a sense of being protected by prayers, sacramentals and so on; and that happiness of this sort satisfies the soul. The Dean, having given us this one ghastly glimpse of the Cardinal's spiritual condition, drops the curtain with a groan and says it is Paganism. How different from the Christian orthodoxy of Plotinus!

Now it was exactly that little glimpse that interested me in this matter; not so much a glimpse into the soul of the Cardinal as into the mind of the Dean. I suddenly seemed to see, in much simpler form than I had yet realised, the real issue between him and us. And the curious thing about the issue is this; that what he thinks about us is exactly what we think about him. What I for one feel most strongly, in considering a case like that of the Dean and his quotation from the Cardinal, is that the Dean is a man of distinguished intelligence and culture, that he is always interesting, that he is sometimes even just, or at least justified or justifiable; but that he is first and last the champion of a Superstition; the man who is really and truly defending a Superstition, as it would be understood by people who could define a Superstition. What makes it all the more amusing is that it is in a rather special sense a Pagan Superstition. But what makes it most intensely interesting, so far as I am concerned, is that the Dean is devoted to what may be called par excellence a superstitious Superstition. I mean that it is in a special sense a LOCAL superstition.

Dean Inge is a superstitious person because he is worshipping a relic; a relic in the sense of a remnant. He is idolatrously adoring the broken fragment of something; simply because that something happens to have lingered out of the past in the place called England; in the rather battered form called Protestant Christianity. It is as if a local patriot were to venerate the statue of Our Lady of Walsingham only because she was in Walsingham and without even remembering that she was in Heaven. It is still more as if he venerated a fragment chipped from the toe of the statue and forgot where it came from and ignored Our Lady altogether. I do not think it superstitious to respect the chip in relation to the statue, or the statue in relation to the saint, or the saint in relation to the scheme of theology and philosophy. But I do think it superstitious to venerate, or even to accept, the fragment because it happens to be there. And Dean Inge does accept the fragment called Protestantism because it happens to be there.

Let us for a moment consider the whole matter as philosophers should; in a universal air above all local superstitions like the Dean's. It is quite obvious that there are three or four philosophies or views of life possible to reasonable men; and to a great extent these are embodied in the great religions or in the wide field of irreligion. There is the atheist, the materialist or monist or whatever he calls himself, who believes that all is ultimately material, and all that is material is mechanical. That is emphatically a view of life; not a very bright or breezy view, but one into which it is quite possible to fit many facts of existence. Then there is the normal man with the natural religion, which accepts the general idea that the world has a design and therefore a designer; but feels the Architect of the Universe to be inscrutable and remote, as remote from men as from microbes. That sort of theism is perfectly sane; and is really the ancient basis of the solid if somewhat stagnant sanity of Islam. There is again the man who feels the burden of life so bitterly that he wishes to renounce all desire and all division, and rejoin a sort of spiritual unity and peace from which (as he thinks) our separate selves should never have broken away. That is the mood answered by buddhism and by many metaphysicians and mystics. Then there is a fourth sort of man, sometimes called a mystic and perhaps more properly to be called a poet; in practice he can very often be called a pagan. His position is this; it is a twilight world and we know not where it ends. If we do not know enough for monotheism, neither do we know enough for monism. There may be a borderland and a world beyond; but we can only catch hints of it as they come; we may meet a nymph in the forest; we may see the fairies on the mountains. We do not know enough about the natural to DENY the preternatural. That was, in ancient times, the healthiest aspect of Paganism. That is, in modern times, the rational part of Spiritualism. All these are possible as general views of life; and there is a fourth that is at least equally possible, though certainly more positive.

The whole point of this last position might be expressed in the line of M. Cammaerts's beautiful little poem about bluebells; LE CIEL EST TOMBE PAR TERRE. Heaven has DESCENDED into the world of matter; the supreme spiritual power is now operating by the machinery of matter, dealing miraculously with the bodies and souls of men. It blesses all the five senses; as the senses of the baby are blessed at a Catholic christening. It blesses even material gifts and keepsakes, as with relics or rosaries. It works through water or oil or bread or wine. Now that sort of mystical materialism may please or displease the Dean, or anybody else. But I cannot for the life of me understand why the Dean, or anybody else, does not SEE that the Incarnation is as much a part of that idea as the Mass; and that the Mass is as much a part of that idea as the Incarnation. A Puritan may think it blasphemous that God should become a wafer. A Moslem thinks it blasphemous that God should become a workman in Galilee. And he is perfectly right, from his point of view; and given his primary principle. But if the Moslem has a principle, the Protestant has only a prejudice. That is, he has only a fragment; a relic; a superstition. If it be profane that the miraculous should descend to the plane of matter, then certainly Catholicism is profane; and Protestantism is profane; and Christianity is profane. Of all human creeds or concepts, in that sense, Christianity is the most utterly profane. But why a man should accept a Creator who was a carpenter, and then worry about holy water, why he should accept a local Protestant tradition that God was born in some particular place mentioned in the Bible, merely because the Bible had been left lying about in England, and then say it is incredible that a blessing should linger on the bones of a saint, why he should accept the first and most stupendous part of the story of Heaven on Earth, and then furiously deny a few small but obvious deductions from it— that is a thing I do not understand; I never could understand; I have come to the conclusion that I shall never understand. I can only attribute it to Superstition.

ON COURAGE AND INDEPENDENCE

WHEN we are pressed and taunted upon our obstinacy in saying the Mass in a dead language, we are tempted to reply to our questioners by telling them that they are apparently not fit to be trusted with a living language. When we consider what they have done with the noble English language, as compared with the English of the Anglican Prayer-Book, let alone the Latin of the Mass, we feel that their development may well be called degenerate.

The language called dead can never be called degenerate. Surely even they might understand our taking refuge in it, by the time that (in the vernacular) the word "immaculate" is applied only to the shirt-fronts of snobs; or "unction" means not Extreme Unction, but only unctuous rectitude. It is needless to note once more how the moral qualities have lost their mystical quality; and with it all their dignity and delicacy and spontaneous spiritual appeal. Charity, that was the flaming heart of the world, has become a name for a niggardly and pompous patronage of the poor, generally amounting by this time to the enslavement of the poor.

But there are more subtle examples of this degeneration in ideal terms. And an even worse example, I think, than the cheapening of the word CHARITY is the new newspaper cheapening of the word COURAGE.

Any man living in complete luxury and security who chooses to write a play or a novel which causes a flutter and exchange of compliments in Chelsea and Chiswick and a faint thrill in Streatham and Surbiton, is described as "daring, " though nobody on earth knows what danger it is that he dares. I speak, of course, of terrestrial dangers; or the only sort of dangers he believes in. To be extravagantly flattered by everybody he considers enlightened, and rather feebly rebuked by everybody he considers dated and dead, does not seem so appalling a peril that a man should be stared at as a heroic warrior and militant martyr because he has had the strength to endure it.

The dramatic critic of a Sunday paper, a little while ago, lashed himself into a frenzy of admiration for the "courage" of some dismal and dirty play or other, because it represented a soldier as raving like a hysterical woman against the cruelty of those who had expected him to defend his country. It may be amusing that his idea of courage should be a defence of cowardice. But it is the sort of defence of it that we have heard ten thousand times during the reaction after the War; and the courage required to utter it is exactly as great as the courage required to utter any other stale quotation from the cant and convention of the moment: such trifles as the absurdity of marriage or the sympathetic personality of Judas Iscariot. These things have become quite commonplace; but they still pretend to be courageous. So sham soldiers have been known to swagger about in uniform when the war was over.

The Catholic Church, as the guardian of all values, guards also the value of words. Her children will not fall, I hope, into this conventional and comfortable folly. We need not pretend that Catholics to-day are called upon to show anything worth calling courage, by the standard of the Catholics in other days. It did require some courage to be a Catholic when it involved the definite disinclination felt by most of us for being racked or ripped up with a knife. It did require some courage when there was only an intermittent possibility of being torn in pieces by a mob. Even that our subtle human psychology regards with some distaste.

But I hope we do not feel any distaste for being on the opposite side to Bishop Barnes, or for being regarded with alarm and suspicion by Jix. These things are almost intellectual pleasures. Indeed, they really involve a certain temptation to intellectual pride. Let us pray to be delivered from it; and let us hope that we are not left altogether without occasions for courage. But most of them will be present in private life and in other practical aspects of public life; in resisting pain or passion or defying the economic threat and tyranny of our time. But do not let us make fools of ourselves like the rationalists and the realists, by posing as martyrs who are never martyred or defying tyrants who have been dead for two hundred years.

But though the name of this virtue has been vulgarized so much that it is hard to use it even where it is exact, let alone where it is in any case exaggerative, there is a somewhat analogous quality which the modern world lauds equally loudly and has lost almost more completely. Putting aside the strict sense of a Catholic courage, the world ought to be told something about Catholic intellectual independence. It is, of course, the one quality which the world supposes that Catholics have lost. It is also, at this moment, the one quality which Catholics perceive that all the world has lost. The modern world has many marks, good as well as bad; but by far the most modern thing in it is the abandonment of individual reason, in favour of press stunts and suggestion and mass psychology and mass production. The Catholic Faith, which always preserves the unfashionable virtue, is at this moment alone sustaining the independent intellect of man.

Our critics, in condemning us, always argue in a circle. They say of mediaevalism that all men were narrow. When they discover that many of them were very broad, they insist that those men must have been in revolt, not only against mediaevalism, but against Catholicism. No Catholics were intelligent; for when they were intelligent, they cannot really have been Catholics. This circular argument appears with a slight difference in the matter of independent thought to-day. It consists of extending to all Catholicism what are in fact the independent ideas of different Catholics. Men start by assuming (what they have been told) that Rome rigidly suppresses ALL variety and therefore Romanists never differ on anything. Then if one of them advances an interesting view, they say that Rome must have imposed it on him and therefore on all the other Roman Catholics. I myself have advanced several economic and political suggestions, for which I never dreamed of claiming anything more than that a loyal Catholic can offer them. But I would rather take any other example than my own unimportant opinions.

In any case, my own experience of the modern world tells me that Catholics are much more and not less individualistic than other men in their general opinions. Mr. Michael Williams, the spirited propagandist of Catholicism in America, gave this as a very cogent reason for refusing to found or join anything like a Catholic party in politics. He said that Catholics will combine for Catholicism, but it is quite abnormally difficult to get them to combine for anything else. This is confirmed by my own impressions and is contrasted very sharply with my recollections about most other religious groups. For instance, what we called the Free Churches, constituting what was also called the Nonconformist Conscience, represented a marvel of moral unity and the spreading of a special spiritual atmosphere. But the Free Churches were not free, whatever else they were. The most striking and even startling thing about them was the ABSENCE of any individual repudiations of the common ideals which the Conscience laid down. The Nonconformist Conscience was not the normal conscience; they would hardly themselves have pretended that the mass of mankind necessarily agreed with them about Drink or Armaments. But they all agreed with each other about Drink or Armaments. A Nonconformist minister standing up to defend public-houses, or public expenditure on guns and bayonets, was a much rarer thing than a heretic in much more hierarchical systems. It was broadly the fact that ALL such men supported what they called Temperance; which seemed to mean an intemperate denunciation of temperate drinking. It is almost as certain that ALL of them insisted on what they called Peace; which seemed, so far as I could make out, to mean such weakening of armament as would involve disaster and destruction in War. But the question here is not whether I disagreed with them; but whether they ever disagreed with each other. And one thing is at least certain, that on things of this sort they disagreed with each other infinitely less than Catholics do. Though the traditional culture and sacramental symbol of the vine makes most Catholics moderately favourable to fermented liquor in moderation, there have been many prominent Catholics who were teetotallers in a degree hardly to be called moderate. The great Cardinal Manning startled all his own supporters by the passion of this private conviction; just as he startled them by many other Radical eccentricities, such as making friends with Stead and championing the Salvation Army. Whether he was right is not here in question; the point is that he thought he was right when his own religious world thought he was wrong, and not unfrequently told him so. You would not have found a man in the Salvation Army to defend Irish whisky, as you found a man like Father Matthew to denounce it.

The same facts could be supported by a hundred facts in my own experience. Dean Inge observed the other day that Mr. Belloc was the only man in England who believed that Dreyfus was guilty. He might have added that he was nearly the only man in England who knew any of the actual facts of the case, which were suppressed in the English newspapers. In any case, the phrase is an exaggeration; for several men, like Lord Chief Justice Russell, whom no one will call incompetent to judge evidence, and old Harry Labouchere, whom no one will call a zealot for militarism, were of the same opinion. But substantially it is true that Mr. Belloc, in the days of his youth, found himself absolutely alone in almost any assembly of English people discussing the question. It is by no means the only occasion on which he has found himself alone. Merely from my own personal knowledge of him, I could give a list as long as this article of topics on which he was opposed to everyone else's opinion and sometimes opposed to mine. To mention only a few things, large and small, he would probably be the only person in a drawing-room saying that Lewis Carroll was overrated, that Byron and Longfellow were not overrated, that wit is superior to humour, that ALLY SLOPE'S HALF-HOLIDAY was superior to PUNCH, that James the Second was chiefly notable as a stolid English patriot suspicious of French influence, that an Irish political murder might actually be as excusable as a Russian political murder (old regime), that half the modern legislation advanced in favour of Labour is part of a plan to re-establish pagan slavery, that it is the mark of the Protestant culture to tolerate Catholicism and the mark of the Catholic culture to persecute it, and a variety of other opinions which would at least be largely regarded as paradoxes. And he says such things because he is a Catholic: which does not mean that other Catholics would say the same. On the contrary, each would say something quite different. It is not that they need agree with him; but that he need not agree with them. Apart from his own genius, Catholics do differ thus more than a company of Anglican public-school patriots or solid Liberal Nonconformists; to say nothing of the middle class of the Middle West, with its rigid pattern of regular guys. Catholics know the two or three transcendental truths on which they do agree; and take rather a pleasure in disagreeing on everything else. A glance at the living literature, written by other Catholics besides Mr. Belloc, will confirm what I say.

I might take, for instance, a book like the remarkable recent work of Mr. Christopher Hollis, "The American Heresy. " Now surely nobody in his senses will say that all Catholics are bound to believe that the Slave States ought to have won the American Civil War, that America ought never to have extended westward of Tennessee, that Andrew Jackson was a savage, or that Abraham Lincoln was a failure, that Calhoun was like a heathen Roman or that Wilson was an arrogant and dishonest schoolmaster. These opinions are not part of the Catholic order; but they are illustrations of the Catholic liberty. And they illustrate exactly the sort of liberty which the modern world emphatically has not got; the real liberty of the mind. It is no longer a question of liberty from kings and captains and inquisitors. It is a question of liberty from catchwords and headlines and hypnotic repetitions and all the plutocratic platitudes imposed on us by advertisement and journalism.

It is strictly true to say that the average reader of the DAILY MAIL and the "Outline of History" is inhibited from these intellectual acts. It is true to say that he CANNOT think that Abraham Lincoln was a failure. It is true to say that he CANNOT think that a Republic should have refused to expand as it has expanded. He cannot move his mind to such a position, even experimentally; it means moving it out of too deep a rut, worn too smooth by the swift traffic of modern talk and journalism, all perpetually moving one way.

These modern people mean by mental activity simply an express train going faster and faster along the same rails to the same station; or having more and more railway carriages hooked on to it to be taken to the same place. The one notion that has vanished from their minds is the notion of voluntary movement even to the same end. They have fixed not only the ends, but the means. They have imposed not only the doctrines, but the words. They are bound not merely in religion, which is avowedly binding, but in everything else as well. There are formal praises of free thought; but even the praises are in a fixed form. Thousands who have never learned to think at all are urged to think whatever may take their fancy about Jesus Christ. But they are, in fact, forbidden to think in any way but one about Abraham Lincoln. That is why it is worth remarking that it is a Catholic who has thought for himself.

THE NORDIC HINDOO

I CANNOT, as some do, find Dr. Barnes a very exciting Bishop merely because he is an Evolutionist in the style of fifty years ago and a Protestant persecutor in the style of eighty years ago. His views are stale enough; but I admit that his arguments are sometimes amusing.

Thus, he reached the last limit of wildness in one remark which he made in the course of explaining that the folklore of the Mediterranean had been forced upon the Nordic nations—whatever that may mean. He added abruptly that Indian and Chinese metaphysics are now much more important than ours. But, above all, he made the crowning assertion that Rome is thus stamped as Provincial. This seems to suggest to the educational mind the construction of an examination paper in elementary general knowledge. It might run something like this:

1. From what language is the word "provincial" derived?

2. To what provinces did it generally refer?

3. If Athens, Antioch, Rome and Jerusalem were provincial towns, what was their Metropolitan city?

4. What reasons are there for supposing that Birmingham occupied this Metropolitan position from the earliest times?

5. Give a short account of the conquest of Southern Europe and the Near East by the Emperors of Birmingham.

6. At what date did the Papacy rebel against the Diocese of Birmingham?

7. Explain the old proverb, "All roads lead to Birmingham."

8. Discuss the following remark, "The most charmingly Nordic people I know are those dear Chinamen."

9. Why is the folklore of the Hindoos so much more reasonable than that of the Romans?

10. When will the Bishop of Birmingham go touring in the Provinces?

Answers must be sent in before the time of the Disestablishment of the Church of England, and priests are forbidden to give their crafty assistance to the candidates.

Really, I do not know any other way of dealing with even a pretence of seriousness with such an extraordinary remark. It was rendered even more extraordinary, of course, by the further remarks on the subject of Chinamen and Hindoos. Now we know all about the Nordic Man, so far as anybody can know anything about a person who does not exist. We know, for instance, that up to the autumn of 1914 he used to be called the Teutonic Man. Dean Inge used to be frightfully fond of him in those days; even fonder than he is now. He once quoted lavishly, and still quotes occasionally, from that great and glorious English patriot, Mr. Houston Stewart Chamberlain.

We quite understood that all Nordic Men were like gods, having long golden hair and gigantic stature; and this made it all the more pleasant to realize that we ourselves were Nordic Men, Unfortunately, the Germans were even more Nordic and gigantic and beautiful to gaze upon; they said so; and they ought to know. The poor Teuton was a little unpopular for five years or so; but now he is creeping out again to feel the sun, like the kings after Napoleon's fall in Mrs. Browning's poem. Like several other people, he changed his name during the War. He is now entirely Nordic and not at all Teutonic. And, as it is, and always was, his whole profession in life to praise himself and exalt the virtue of pride, so much undervalued by Christians, it is perfectly natural that he should despise "Dagos" and talk about the lower culture of lesser breeds without the law. It is natural that he should insist that all Spaniards are cowardly bullfighters and all Italians luxurious organ-grinders. He may be expected to point out at intervals the sluggish incompetence of Napoleon and the impotent languor of Mussolini.

All this we were used to; it was what we expected from the Nordic Man; for nobody ever expected a Nordic Man to face facts staring him in the face, or to learn anything even from his own experience. We thought we had it all clear and complete, like a mutual understanding; there was the Nordic Man who was noble because he was Protestant and had light hair; and there was the Southern Catholic who was a lower sort of animal, because he was swarthy and superstitious. But why Hindoos? 0 Venerable Father in God and gentle shepherd of souls, why Hindoos?

Why are we now told to learn from people who are even less light-haired and even further off from the Arctic Circle? Are they not a lower race, conquered by the earth-shaking Imperialism of Birmingham? Are they not a lesser breed without the law? Are we to go to Asia to escape from the folklore and magic? Do the dear Indians never exhibit any of the errors that deface the deplorable Romans? If the Latins are idolaters, do the Indians never have idols? If Southern Europe is attached to mythology, is Southern Asia a world of pure reason that has never been defaced by a myth?

The explanation, the only explanation that I can suggest, is the one I have already suggested; and it is in a simple word; the word DESPAIR. Everybody knows that when a military campaign begins to fail there is an inevitable and even pardonable temptation to every military commander on the defeated side to lower the standard of military fitness and collect soldiers from anywhere, whatever be their military quality. This has happened again and again even among the white races; something similar is constantly happening in their relation to the other races. So both the Dutch and the English in the South African quarrel have been continually tempted to make use of the natives for war as well as labour. France has been blamed for relying on dark troops; though I never could see why she should be blamed by us, who drew dark troops from all over our own Empire.

Anyhow, it is a process that defeated or embarrassed captains fall back upon regularly but often reluctantly. It is a very exact parallel to the defeat of the Bishop of Birmingham and his cry for help to the Hindoos. He has reached the position in which he will accept reinforcements from anywhere except Rome. Rome must be provincial; even if it is the only place in the world that is provincial. Rome must be barbaric; if all the barbarians of the earth are called up to sack the city.

And when we have reached that point, it is not difficult to see that the very invasion and spoliation proclaim it to be a Holy City; unique and universal and towering over the tribes of men.

A SPIRITUALIST LOOKS BACK

WE hear much about new religions; many of them based on the very latest novelties of Buddha and Pythagoras. But I have come to a conclusion which I fear will offend still more. I fancy that all modern religions are counter-religions; attacks on, or alternative to the Catholic Church. They bear no likeness to the natural pagan speculations that existed before the Catholic Church, or would exist if it had never existed. The attitude of Dean Inge is certainly much more like that of Plotinus than that of Plato. But it is even more like that of Porphyry than that of Plotinus. He is exactly like some pagan of the decline; it is not necessary for him to know very much about the Christian superstition; as soon as he heard of it, he hated it.

In a recent work, which I have considered in this place, he is careful to insist that the word PROTESTANT had an old meaning which was not merely negative. And he has certainly fulfilled an old meaning that is positive; if the word Protestant means a man who doth protest too much. He is so very anxious to explain what he thinks about the Catholic Church that he cannot keep it out of any article about M. Coue or Monkey Glands.

The Dean stands by himself; and must be presumably described as an Anglican, for want of anything else in particular to call him. But it is very interesting to observe that even those who seem to go out into the wilderness to stake out their own Promised Land, like the Mormons, are eventually found to be as much a mere reaction against orthodoxy as the Modernists. Their march towards the new Utopia is found to be only a rather longer and more elaborate manoeuvre of one of the armies besieging the Holy City. We imagined that these new schismatics had finally gone off to pray; but we always find (a little while afterwards) that they have remained to scoff. They always come back to boo and riot in our churches when they have got tired of trying to build their own.

One who thus reveals all that he does not know, and certainly ought to know, is Sir Arthur Conan Doyle. He broke out the other day into a diatribe, which was supposed to begin with the relations of his new religion to others, but which turned with incalculable rapidity into mere abuse of his old original family religion, as if there were no other in the world.

Perhaps he is right; and there is not. But you would think a man fresh from founding a new religion might have a few new things to say about that; instead of old and negative things to say about something else. But the special strictures of Sir Arthur Conan Doyle on Catholic orthodoxy had a certain very curious character, which alone makes them worth noting at all. In themselves they are almost indescribably stale and thin and shabby; and have been thrashed threadbare in a hundred controversies. But the odd thing which I want to remark about them is this; that they are not only old, but old-fashioned, in the sense that they do not even fit into what is now fashionable. They had some meaning sixty years ago. They have no meaning at all for anybody who looks at the living world as it is— even at the world of new faiths or fads like Spiritualism. But the Spiritualist is not looking even at the Spiritualist world. He is not looking at the human world, or the heathen world, or even at the worldly world. He is looking only at the thing he hates.

For instance, he says, exactly as did our Calvinist great-grandmother, that the Confessional is a most indelicate institution; and that it is highly improper for a young lady of correct deportment, in the matter of prunes and prisms, to mention such things as sins to a strange gentleman who is a celibate. Well, of course, all Catholics know the answer to that; and hundreds of Catholics have answered it to Protestants who had some sort of right or reason to ask it.

Nobody, or next to nobody, has ever had to go into so much morbid detail in confessing to a priest as in confessing to a doctor. And the joke of it is that the Protestant great-grandmother, who objected to the gentleman priest, would have been the very first to object to a lady doctor. What matters in the confessional is the moral guilt and not the material details. But the material details are everything in medicine, even for the most respectable and responsible physician, let alone all the anarchical quacks who have been let loose to hear confessions in the name of Psychoanalysis or Hypnotic Cures. But though we all know the old and obvious answers, what I find startling is this: that our critic does not see the new and obvious situation.

What in the world is the sense of his coming with his prunes and prisms into the sort of society that surrounds us to-day? If a girl must not mention sin to a man in a corner of a church, it is apparently the only place nowadays in which she may not do so. She may sit side by side with him on a jury and discuss the details of the foulest and most perverted wickedness in the world, perhaps with a man's life hanging on the minuteness of the detail. She may read in novels and newspapers sins she has never heard of, let alone sins she is likely to commit or confess. She must not whisper to an impersonal presence behind a grating the most abstract allusion to the things that she hears shouted and cat-called in all the theatrical art and social conversation of the day.

Sir Arthur Conan Doyle must know as well as I do that modesty of that sort is not being regarded at all by the modern world; and that nobody dreams of attempting to safeguard it so strictly as it is safeguarded in Catholic conversation and Catholic confessions. We can say of Rome and Purity what Swinburne said, in another sense, about Rome and Liberty — "Who is against but all her men, and who is beside her but Thou? " And yet the critic has the impudence to accuse us of the neglect of what all but we are neglecting; simply because that charge was used against us a century ago, and anything used against us can be used over and over again, until it drops to pieces. The old stick of the old grandmother is still good enough to beat the old dog with, though if the old grandmother could rise from the dead, she would think the dog the only decent object in the landscape.

I mean nothing flippant when I say that the only interesting thing about all this is its staleness. I have no unfriendly feelings towards Sir Arthur Conan Doyle, to whom we all owe so much gratitude in the realm of literature and entertainment, and who often seems to me entirely right in his manner of defending Spiritualism against Materialism. But I do realize, even if he does not realize, that, at the back of the whole business, he is not defending Spiritualism, and not attacking Materialism; he is attacking Rome.

By a deep and true ancestral instinct with him, he knows that this is ultimately the one Thing to be either attacked or defended; and that he that is not against it is for it. Unless the claim of the Church can be challenged in the modern world, it is impossible really to set up an alternative modern religion. He feels that to be a fact, and I am glad to sympathize with him. Indeed, it is because I would remain so far sympathetic that I take only one example among the doctrines he denounced; and deliberately avoid, for instance, his strangely benighted remarks on the cult of the Blessed Virgin. For I confess to a difficulty in remaining patient with blindness about that topic. But there are other parallel topics.

He has some very innocent remarks about what he considers grotesque in the sacramental system; innocent, because apparently unconscious of what everybody else in the world considers grotesque in the spiritualistic system. If any Christian service was so conducted as to resemble a really successful seance, the world might well be excused for falling back on the word "grotesque, " a favourite word of Dr. Watson. Indeed, we may well question whether the institution of the Red-Headed League or the episode of the Yellow Face at the window, or any of the fantasies of Mr. Sherlock Holmes, were any more fantastic than some that have been submitted to us seriously enough by the school of Sir Arthur Conan Doyle. I do not say that this test of external extravagance ought to be final, or that no defence of such details could be made. But when Sir Arthur deliberately gibes at our ceremonies, we may at least be allowed to smile at his. Suppose any Catholic rite before the altar consisted of binding a human being hand and foot with ropes; should we ever hear the last of the horrible survival of human sacrifice? Suppose we declared that the priest went into a trance and that clouds of thick white stuff like cotton-wool came out of his mouth, as a manifestation of celestial grace; might not some of our critics be heard to murmur the word, "grotesque"? If we conducted a quiet little evening service in which a big brass trumpet careered about in the air and patted people on the head, caressed a lady with intimate gestures of affection, and generally exhibited itself as about as attractive an object as a philandering trombone or an amorous big drum, would not our critics have something to say about the unwholesome hysteria and senseless excitement of Popery? If the Spiritualist goes out of his way to challenge us to a duel in the matter of dignity, I do not really think it can be reasonably said that he is on stronger ground than we.

But I remark on all these charges, not in order to show how they recoil upon themselves, but in order to show how the Spiritualist is driven to return upon himself, and to react against his origins, and to forget all else in making war upon his mother.

The man of the modern religion does not quarrel with the modern world, as he well might, for its neglect of modesty. He quarrels with the ancient mother, who is alone teaching it any modesty at all. He does not devote himself to condemning the modern dances or the fashionable comedies for their vulgar and obvious indifference to dignity. He brings his special charge of grotesque extravagance against the only ceremonial that really retains any dignity. It seems to him, somehow, more important that the Catholic Church should be, on the most minute point, open to misunderstanding, than that the whole world should go to the devil in a dance of death before his very eyes. And he is quite right; at least, the instinct of which this is a symbol is quite right.

The world really pays the supreme compliment to the Catholic Church in being intolerant of her tolerating even the appearance of the evils which it tolerates in everything else. A fierce light does indeed beat upon that throne and blacken every blot; but the interest here is in the fact that even those who profess to be setting up new thrones or throwing new light are perpetually looking backwards at the original blaze if only to discover the blots. They have not really succeeded in getting out of the orbit of the system which they criticize. They have not really found new stars; they are still pointing at alleged spots on the sun, and thereby admitting that it is their native daylight and the centre of their solar system.

THE ROOTS OF SANITY

THE Dean of St. Paul's, when he is right, is very right. He is right with all that ringing emphasis that makes him in other matters so rashly and disastrously wrong. And I cannot but hail with gratitude the scorn with which he spoke lately of all the newspaper nonsense about using monkey-glands to turn old men into young men; or into young monkeys, if that is to be the next step towards the Superman. Not unnaturally, he tried to balance his denunciation of that very experimental materialism which he is always accusing us of denouncing, by saying that this materialism is one evil extreme and that Catholicism is the other. In that connection he said some of the usual things which he commonly finds it easy to say, and we generally find it tolerably easy to answer.

For instance, it is a good example of the contradictory charges brought against Rome that the Dean apparently classes us with those who leave children entirely "unwarned" about the moral dangers of the body. Considering that we have been abused for decades on the ground that we forced on the young the infamous suggestions of the Confessional, this is rather funny.

Only the other day I noted that Sir Arthur Conan Doyle revived this charge of an insult to innocence; and I will leave Dean Inge and Sir Arthur to fight it out. And when he charges us with indifference to Eugenics and the breeding of criminals and lunatics, it is enough that he has himself to denounce the perversion of science manifested in the monkey business. He might permit others to resent equally the schemes by which men are to act like lunatics and criminals in order to avoid lunacy and crime.

There is, however, another aspect of this matter of being right or wrong, which is not so often associated with us, but which is equally consistent with our philosophy. And it has a notable bearing on the sort of questions here raised by Dean Inge. It concerns not only the matters in which the world is wrong, but rather especially the matters in which the world is right. The world, especially the modern world, has reached a curious condition of ritual or routine; in which we might almost say that it is wrong even when it is right. It continues to a great extent to do the sensible things. It is rapidly ceasing to have any of the sensible reasons for doing them. It is always lecturing us on the deadness of tradition; and it is living entirely on the life of tradition. It is always denouncing us for superstition; and its own principal virtues are now almost entirely superstitions.

I mean that when we are right, we are right by principle; and when they are right, they are right by prejudice. We can say, if they prefer it so, that they are right by instinct. But anyhow, they are still restrained by healthy prejudice from many things into which they might be hurried by their own unhealthy logic. It is easiest to take very simple and even extreme examples; and some of the extremes are nearer to us than some may fancy.

Thus, most of our friends and acquaintances continue to entertain a healthy prejudice against Cannibalism. The time when this next step in ethical evolution will be taken seems as yet far distant. But the notion that there is not very much difference between the bodies of men and animals—that is not by any means far distant, but exceedingly near. It is expressed in a hundred ways, as a sort of cosmic communism. We might almost say that it is expressed in every other way except cannibalism.

It is expressed, as in the Voronoff notion, in putting pieces of animals into men. It is expressed, as in the vegetarian notion, in not putting pieces of animals into men. It is expressed in letting a man die as a dog dies, or in thinking it more pathetic that a dog should die than a man. Some are fussy about what happens to the bodies of animals, as if they were quite certain that a rabbit resented being cooked, or that an oyster demanded to be cremated. Some are ostentatiously indifferent to what happens to the bodies of men; and deny all dignity to the dead and all affectionate gesture to the living. But all these have obviously one thing in common; and that is that they regard the human and bestial body as common things. They think of them under a common generalisation; or under conditions at best comparative. Among people who have reached this position, the REASON for disapproving of cannibalism has already become very vague. It remains as a tradition and an instinct. Fortunately, thank God, though it is now very vague, it is still very strong. But though the number of earnest ethical pioneers who are likely to begin to eat boiled missionary is very small, the number of those among them who could explain their own real reason for not doing so is still smaller.

The real reason is that all such social sanities are now the traditions of old Catholic dogmas. Like many other Catholic dogmas, they are felt in some vague way even by heathens, so long as they are healthy heathens. But when it is a question of their not being merely felt but formulated, it will be found to be a formula of the Faith. In this case it is all those ideas that Modernists most dislike, about "special creation" and that Divine image that does not come merely by evolution, and the chasm between man and the other creatures. In short, it is those very doctrines with which men like Dean Inge are perpetually reproaching us, as things that forbid us a complete confidence in science or a complete unity with animals. It is these that stand between men and cannibalism—or possibly monkey glands. They have the prejudice; and long may they retain it! We have the principle, and they are welcome to it when they want it.

If Euclid were demonstrating with diagrams for the first time and used the argument of the REDUCTIO AD ABSURDUM, he would now only produce the impression that his own argument was absurd. I am well aware that I expose myself to this peril by extending my opponent's argument to an extreme, which may be considered an extravagance. The question is, why is it an extravagance? I know that in this case it will be answered that the social feature of cannibalism is rare in our culture. So far as I know, there are no cannibal restaurants threatening to become fashionable in London like Chinese restaurants. Anthropophagy is not like Anthroposophy, a subject of society lectures; and, varied as are the religions and moralities among us, the cooking of missionaries is not yet a mission. But if anyone has so little of logic as to miss the meaning of an extreme example, I should have no difficulty in giving a much more practical and even pressing example. A few years ago, all sane people would have said that Adamitism was quite as mad as Anthropophagy. A banker walking down the streets with no clothes on would have been quite as nonsensical as a butcher selling man instead of mutton. Both would be the outbreak of a lunatic under the delusion that he was a savage. But we have seen the New Adamite or No Clothes Movement start quite seriously in Germany; start indeed with a seriousness of which only Germans are capable. Englishmen probably are still English enough to laugh at it and dislike it. But they laugh by instinct; and they only dislike by instinct. Most of them, with their present muddled moral philosophy, would probably have great difficulty in refuting the Prussian professor of nakedness, however heartily they might desire to kick him. For if we examine the current controversies, we shall find the same negative and defenceless condition as in the case of the theory of cannibalism. All the fashionable arguments used against Puritanism do in fact lead to Adamitism. I do not mean, of course, that they are not often practically healthy as against Puritanism; still less do I mean that there are no better arguments against Puritanism. But I mean that in pure logic the civilised man has laid open his guard; and is, as it were, naked against the inroads of nakedness. So long as he is content merely to argue that the body is beautiful or that what is natural is right, he has surrendered to the Adamite in theory, though it may be, please God, a long time before he surrenders in practice. Here again the modern theorist will have to defend his own sanity with a prejudice. It is the mediaeval theologian who can defend it with a reason. I need not go into that reason at length; it is enough to say that it is founded on the Fall of Man, just as the other instinct against cannibalism is founded on the Divinity of Man. The Catholic argument can be put shortly by saying that there is nothing the matter with the human body; what is the matter is with the human soul.

In other words, if man were completely a god, it might be true that all aspects of his bodily being were godlike; just as if he were completely a beast, we could hardly blame him for any diet, however beastly. But we say that experience confirms our theory of his human complexity. It has nothing to do with the natural things themselves. If red roses mysteriously maddened men to commit murder, we should make rules to cover them up; but red roses would be quite as pure as white ones.

In most modern people there is a battle between the new opinions, which they do not follow out to their end, and the old traditions, which they do not trace back to their beginning. If they followed the new notions forward, it would lead them to Bedlam. If they followed the better instincts backward, it would lead them to Rome. At the best they remain suspended between two logical alternatives, trying to tell themselves, as does Dean Inge, that they are merely avoiding two extremes. But there is this great difference in his case, that the question on which he is wrong is, in however perverted a form, a matter of science, whereas the matter in which he is right is by this time simply a matter of sentiment. I need not say that I do not use the word here in a contemptuous sense, for in these things there is a very close kinship between sentiment and sense. But the fact remains that all the people in his position can only go on being sensible. It is left for us to be also reasonable.

SOME OF OUR ERRORS

THE thoughtful reader, studying the literature of the enlightened and scientific when they advise us about ethics and religion, will be arrested by one phrase which really has a meaning. Nay, he will observe, with increasing interest and excitement, that it really contains a truth. Most of the phrases that are supposed to go along with it, and to be of the same sort, will be found to be not only untrue but almost unmeaning. When the Modernist says that we must free the human intellect from the mediaeval syllogism, it is as if he said we must free it from the multiplication-table. Some people can count or reason quicker than others; some people put in all the steps and are safe; some people leave out the steps and are still right; many leave out the steps and are consequently wrong. But the process of multiplication is the same, and the process of demonstration is the same. Men think in that way, except when they escape from it by ceasing to think. Or again, when we find in the same context the remark that some Christian doctrine which we do know is "only a form of" some Pagan cult that nobody really knows, we realise that the mathematician is treating the unknown quantity as the known. But when we find among these fallacies the remark I speak of, we shall be wise to pause upon it with greater patience. It is the remark, "We need a restatement of religion"; and though it has been said thirty thousand times, it is quite true.

It is also true that those who say it often mean the very opposite of what they say. As I have remarked elsewhere, they very often intend not to restate anything, but to state something else, introducing as many of the old words as possible. By this time not only the word religion, but also the word restatement, is becoming rather an old word. But anyhow the point is that they do not really mean that we should give freshness and a new aspect to religion by calling it roly-poly or rumpti-foo. On the contrary, they mean that we should take something totally different and agree to call it religion. I mention, with some sadness, that I have said this before; because I have found it quite difficult to get them to see a fact of almost heart-breaking simplicity. It seems to strike them as being merely a fine shade of distinction; but it strikes me as a rather grotesque and staggering reversal. There would be the same fine shade of difference, if somebody of a sartorial sort came to me protesting that my aged father was waiting in rags on my door-step, and urgently needing a new hat and coat, and indeed a complete equipment; if he made the most animated preparations for the reclothing of my parent, and the whole episode ended by his introducing me to a total stranger begging for my father's old hat.

Now I do really believe that there is a need for the restatement of religious truth; but not the statement of something quite different, which I do not believe to be true. I believe there is a very urgent need for a verbal paraphrase of many of the fundamental doctrines; simply because people have ceased to understand them as they are traditionally stated. It does not follow from this that the traditional statement is not the true statement. It only means that the traditional statement now needs to be translated; although translation is seldom true. This is especially the case in connection with Catholic ideas; because they were originally stated in what some call a dead language and some an everlasting language. But anyhow, they were stated in a language that has since broken up into other languages, and mixed with other dialects, and produced a popular PATOIS which is spirited, and often splendid, but necessarily less exact. Now I do think that the Catholic culture suffers very much from the popular misunderstanding of its original terminology. I do think that Catholics are themselves to blame, in many cases, for not realising that their doctrines need to be stated afresh, and not left in language that is intrinsically correct but practically misleading. Those who call themselves liberal, commonly take for granted that the fault is with a dead language, as against a language that has developed. If they were really liberal, they could enlarge their minds to see that there is a case for the language having degenerated. But in either case, it is practically true that there are misunderstandings, and that we ought chiefly to desire to make people understand. And I think we have faults and follies of our own in this matter; and that it is not always the fault of our enemies that they misunderstand. There are cases in which we, more or less unconsciously, misinform them. We do not allow enough, in justifying the words that we speak, for the difference in the words that they hear. And I propose to say a few words in this article upon what I may call Catholic criticisms of Catholic faults; or what are (in many cases) merely Catholic accidents and misunderstanding.

For instance, there is a sort of misunderstanding that is simply mistranslation. Probably we have never properly explained to them the real case for using Latin for something that must be immutable and universal. But as half of them are howling day and night for an international language, and accepting a journalese jibberish with plurals in "oj" because they can get no better, some glimmering of the old use of Latin by Erasmus or Bacon might reasonably be expected of them. Of the full defence of such a hieratic tongue I may say something later. But for the moment I am thinking of certain mistakes which arise very largely by our fault and not theirs. It is not the Church's Latin that is to blame; it is the English Catholic's English. It is not because we do not translate it into the vulgar tongue that we are wrong; it is because we do. Sometimes, I am sorry to say, we translate it into a very vulgar tongue. When we do translate things into English, they often only serve as a luminous argument for leaving them in Latin. Latin is Latin, and always says exactly what it means. But popular versions of Latin things often only serve to make them unpopular.

I will venture to take one example, about which I feel very strongly. Will somebody with better authority than I have announce in a voice of thunder, through a trumpet or with a salute of big guns, the vital and very much needed truth that "dulcis" is not the Latin for "sweet"? "Sweet" is not the English word for "dulcis"; any more than for "doux" or "douce. " It has a totally different connotation and atmosphere. "Dulce et decorum est pro patria mori" does not mean "it is sweet and decorous to die for our country. " It means something untranslatable like everything that means anything; but something more like "It is a gracious thing and of good report to die for our country. " When Roland was dying in the mountains, having blown his horn and broken his sword, and thought of "La doulce France" and the men of his line, he did not sully his lips by saying "sweet France, " but something like "beautiful and gracious France. " In English the word "sweet" has been rendered hopelessly sticky by the accident of the word "sweets. " But in any case it suggests something much more intense and even pungent in sweetness like the tabloids of saccharine that are of concentrated sugar. It is at once too strong and too weak a word. It has not the same savour as the same word in the Latin languages, which often means no more than the word "gentle" as it was used of "a perfect gentle knight. " But English Catholicism, having in the great calamity of our history gone into exile in the sixteenth and seventeenth centuries (at the very moment when our modern language was being finally made) naturally had to seek for its own finest enthusiasms in foreign languages. It could not find a salutation to the Mass or the Blessed Virgin except in French or Italian or Spanish or some such tongue; and it translated these things back into a language with which the exile had lost touch and in which his taste was not quite firm and sure. It seemed to be thought necessary to use the word "sweet" in every single case of the kind; which produces not only something that did not sound English; but something which did not sound in the least as the Latin or French sounded. In a certain number of cases, of course, it is exactly the right word; just as it is from time to time in ordinary English poetry. Sometimes it is right because it is so obviously the natural and inevitable word that it would seem more affected not to use it than to use it; as in the song of Burns; "My love is like the melody that's sweetly played in tune. " Sometimes it is right because there is something to be a salt to its sweetness, as in Sir Philip Sidney's line; "Before the eyes of that sweet enemy France. " Similarly it is often exactly right in good Catholic translations or compositions in English. But this fixed notion that it must always be used wherever some such tender expression would be used in Romance literature is simply a blunder in translation; and a blunder that has had very bad effects in fields much more important than literature. I believe that this incongruous and inaccurate repetition of the word "sweet" has kept more Englishmen out of the Catholic Church than all the poison of the Borgias or all the poisonous lies of the people who have written about them.

Ours is at this moment the most rational of all religions. It is even, in a sense, the most rationalistic of all religions. Those who talk about it as merely or mainly emotional simply do not know what they are talking about. It is all the other religions, all the modern religions, that are merely emotional. This is as true of the emotional salvationism of the first Protestants as of the emotional intuitionalism of the last Modernists. We alone are left accepting the action of the reason and the will, without any necessary assistance from the emotions. A convinced Catholic is easily the most hard-headed and logical person walking about the world to-day. But this old slander, of a slimy sentimentalism in all we say and do, is terribly perpetuated by this mere muddle about words. We are still supposed to have a silly sort of devotion, when we really have the most sensible sort, merely because we have taken a foreign phrase and translated it wrong; instead of either leaving it in Latin for those who can read Latin or trusting it in English to people who can write English. But if in this case we admit that the misunderstanding is more our fault than our opponents' fault, the fault which we confess is the very reverse of the fault of which the opponents complain. It has not arisen through the Catholic practice of saying prayers in Latin. On the contrary, it has arisen through the Protestant practice of always saying them in English. It has come through yielding merely weakly and mechanically to the Protestant pressure in the days when our tradition was completely out of fashion. In other words, it has come through doing exactly what they advised us to do, and not doing it well. Of course I do not mean that it is not a good thing to have good popular translation when it is done well. I think it is a very good thing indeed. But while I see what there is to be said for the cult of the vernacular, the Protestant critic does not see what there is to be said for the fixed form of the classic tongue. He does not see that there is something to be said even for the general idea that Catholic poetry should be in the vernacular like the Divine Comedy and Catholic worship in the fundamental language like the Mass.

It is a question between a dead language and a dying language. Every living language is a dying language, even if it does not die. Parts of it are perpetually perishing or changing their sense; there is only one escape from that flux; and a language must die to be immortal. The style of the English Jacobean translation is as noble and simple a thing as any in the world; but even there the words degenerate. It is not their fault; but ours who misuse them; but they are misused. No language could lift itself into a loftier or simpler strain than that which begins, "Comfort ye, comfort ye my people"; but even then, when we pass on to "speak ye comfortably to Jerusalem, " we stumble over a word we have vulgarised.

But the world plays havoc with all such words, whether they are in the English Bible or the Latin Canon. There are many words of Catholic usage which have in practice been thus misused. When an outsider hears that a Catholic has refrained from something for fear of "causing scandal, " he instantly has an irritated impression that it means a fear of setting all the silly old women in the town talking gossip. Of course it means nothing of the kind. It does not mean that in Greek. It does not mean that in Latin. It ought not to mean that in English. It ought to mean what it says; the fear of tripping somebody up, of putting a stumbling-block in the way of some struggling human being. If I encourage to carousals a man who must be kept off drink, I am causing scandal. If I talk what might be a wholesome realism for some hearers, to a young and innocent person who is certain to feel it as mere obscenity, I am causing scandal. I am doing what for me is right, at the risk of making him do what for him is wrong. To say that that is unjustifiable is manifest moral common sense. But it is not conveyed in modern English by talking about causing scandal. All that is conveyed in modern English is that the person so acting is disdaining idle chatter and irresponsible criticism; which is exactly what all the saints and martyrs have consistently lived and died by doing. And that is a good example of what I mean by translation; or, if the word be preferred, by restatement. But that does not mean turning round and abusing the old statement, which was really quite correctly stated. It only means restating exactly what the old statement states.

I could give many other examples of words which were right in their Latin use, but which have become obscured in their English misuse. I always feel it in the necessarily frequent phrase "offending" God; which had originally almost the awful meaning of wounding God. But the word has degenerated through its application to man, until the sound of it is quite petty and perverted. We say that Mr. Binks was quite offended or that Aunt Susan will take offence; and lose sight of the essential truth, and even dogma that (in that lower sense) God is the very last to take offence. But here again we should not abuse the Latin language; we should abuse our own vulgarisation of the English language. Upon this one point, of the restatement of religious ideas, the reformers are right in everything except the one essential; which is knowing where to throw the blame.

THE SLAVERY OF THE MIND

I HAVE chosen the subject of the slavery of the mind because I believe many worthy people imagine I am myself a slave. The nature of my supposed slavery I need not name and do not propose specially to discuss. It is shared by every sane man when he looks up a train in Bradshaw. That is, it consists in thinking a certain authority reliable; which is entirely reasonable. Indeed it would be rather difficult to travel in every train to find out where it went. It would be still more difficult to go to the destination in order to discover whether it was safe to begin the journey. Suppose a wild scare arose that Bradshaw was a conspiracy to produce railway accidents, a man might still believe the Guide to be a Guide and the scare to be only a scare; but he would know of the existence of the scare. What I mean by the slavery of the mind is that state in which men do not know of the alternative. It is something which clogs the imagination, like a drug or a mesmeric sleep, so that a person cannot possibly think of certain things at all. It is not the state in which he says, "I see what you mean; but I cannot think that because I sincerely think this" (which is simply rational): it is one in which he has never thought of the other view; and therefore does not even know that he has never thought of it. Though I am not discussing here my own religion, I think it only right to say that its authorities have never had this sort of narrowness. You may condemn their condemnations as oppressive; but not in this sense as obscurantist. St. Thomas Aquinas begins his enquiry by saying in effect, "Is there a God? It would seem not, for the following reasons"; and the most criticised of recent Encyclicals always stated a view before condemning it. The thing I mean is a man's inability to state his opponent's view; and often his inability even to state his own.

Curiously enough, I find this sort of thing rather specially widespread in our age, which claims to possess a popular culture or enlightenment. There is everywhere the habit of assuming certain things, in the sense of not even imagining the opposite things. For instance, as history is taught, nearly everybody assumes that in all important past conflicts, it was the right side that won. Everybody assumes it; and nobody knows that he assumes it. The man has simply never seriously entertained the other notion. Say to him that we should now all of us be better off if Charles Edward and the Jacobites had captured London instead of falling back from Derby, and he will laugh. He will think it is what he calls a "paradox. " Yet nothing can be a more sober or solid fact than that, when the issue was undecided, wise and thoughtful men were to be found on both sides; and the Jacobite theory is not in any way disproved by the fact that Cumberland could outflank the clans at Drummossie. I am not discussing whether it was right as a theory; I am only noting that it is never allowed to occur to anybody as a thought. The things that might have been are not even present to the imagination. If somebody says that the world would now be better if Napoleon had never fallen, but had established his Imperial dynasty, people have to adjust their minds with a jerk. The very notion is new to them. Yet it would have prevented the Prussian reaction; saved equality and enlightenment without a mortal quarrel with religion; unified Europeans and perhaps avoided the Parliamentary corruption and the Fascist and Bolshevist revenges. But in this age of free-thinkers, men's minds are not really free to think such a thought.

What I complain of is that those who accept the verdict of fate in this way accept it without knowing why. By a quaint paradox, those who thus assume that history always took the right turning are generally the very people who do not believe there was any special providence to guide it. The very rationalists who jeer at the trial by combat, in the old feudal ordeal, do in fact accept a trial by combat as deciding all human history. In the war of the North and South in America, some of the Southern rebels wrote on their flags the rhyme, "Conquer we must for our cause is just. " The philosophy was faulty; and in that sense it served them right that their opponents copied and continued it in the form "Conquer they didn't; so their cause wasn't. " But the latter logic is as bad as the former. I have just read a book called, "The American Heresy, " by Mr. Christopher Hollis. It is a very brilliant and original book; but I know it will not be taken sufficiently seriously; because the reader will have to wrench his mind out of a rut even to imagine the South victorious; still more to imagine anybody saying that a small, limited and agricultural America would have been better for everybody—especially Americans.

I could give many other examples of what I mean by this imaginative bondage. It is to be found in the strange superstition of making sacred figures out of certain historical characters; who must not be moved from their stiff symbolic attitudes. Even their bad qualities are sacred. Much new light has lately been thrown on Queen Elizabeth and Mary Stuart. It is not only favourable to Mary but on the whole favourable to Elizabeth. It seems pretty certain that

Mary did not plot to kill Darnley. It seems highly probable that Elizabeth did not plot to kill Mary. But many people are quite as tenderly attached to the idea of a merciless Elizabeth as to that of a murderous Mary. That a man devoted to Protestantism should rejoice that Elizabeth succeeded, that a man devoted to Catholicism should wish that Mary had succeeded—all that would be perfectly natural and rational. But Elizabeth was not Protestantism; and it ought not to disturb anybody to discover that she was hardly a Protestant. It ought to be even less gratification to her supporters to insist that she was a tyrant. But there is a sort of waxwork history, that cannot be happy unless Elizabeth has an axe and Mary a dagger. This sense of fixed and sacred figures ought to belong to a religion; but a historical speculation is not a religion. To believe in Calvinism by faith alone is comprehensible. To believe in Cromwell by faith alone is incomprehensible. It is supremely incomprehensible that when Calvinists left off believing in Calvinism, they still insisted on believing in Cromwell. To a simple rationalist like myself, these prejudices are hard to understand.

INGE VERSUS BARNES

NONE of us I hope ever wished to be unjust to Dean Inge: though in such fights the button will sometimes come off the foil. And a cruel injustice is being done to him, in the suggestion widely circulated that he agrees with Dr. Barnes. Such things should not be lightly said of any gentleman. It is in accordance with the current legend, at least, that the Gloomy Dean even when he comes to bless should remain to curse. But if there is one isolated human being whom he can be imagined as wanting to bless, one would think it would be his ally, Bishop Barnes of Birmingham. And yet the alliance only serves to soften the curse and not to secure the blessing. If we may use such popular terms of such dignified ecclesiastics, we might be tempted to say that the Dean has found it necessary to throw over the Bishop. An interesting review by the Dean of the Bishop's recent book of sermons contains, of course, a certain number of rather conventional compliments and a certain number of rather abrupt sneers, we might say snarls, at various other people including the greater part of Christendom. But on the two striking and outstanding matters on which Bishop Barnes was condemned by the Catholics, he is almost as strongly condemned by the Dean of St. Paul's. Dean Inge is far too intelligent and cultivated a man to pretend to have much patience with the nonsense about testing Transubstantiation either by chemical experiments or psychical research. He tries to break it to his Broad Church colleague as gently as possible that the latter has made himself a laughing stock. But allowing for such necessary politeness between partners, it could hardly be stated better or even more plainly. He curtly refers the Bishop to the responsible definition of the doctrine in Father Rickaby's book on metaphysics; and drily observes that it will be found rather more subtle and plausible than the Bishop seems to be aware of. He also adds, with a grim candour which is rather attractive, that it is pretty disastrous to challenge Catholics about whether the Mass does them any spiritual good, since they would quite certainly unite in testifying that it does. After these frank and arresting admissions, it is a mere matter of routine, and almost of respectability, that the Dean should agree with the Bishop that all such sacramentalism is very deplorable; that the admittedly intelligent people he knows who say they have found Christ in the Mass and not in the Morning Service must be "natural idolaters" and that it is "obvious" that the Blessed Sacrament has an affinity with the lower religions. Also with the lower classes. That, I fancy, is what the Dean really finds so disgusting about it.

The point is, however, that the Dean definitely snubs the Bishop on the one great point on which the newspapers have boomed and boosted him. And he does exactly the same thing, if in a lesser degree, on the second and lesser matter which was similarly boosted. I mean, of course, the matter of Evolution. The Dean, of course, believes in Evolution, as do a good many other people, Catholic and Protestant as well as agnostic. But though he believes in Evolution, he does not believe in Bishop Barnes's Evolution. He comments with admirable clarity and decision on the folly of identifying progress with evolution; or even mere complication with progress. Nothing could be better than the brief and brisk sentences in which he disposes altogether of that idealisation of the scientific theory, which is in fact simply ignorance of it. In plain words, Bishop Barnes, for all his bluster, knows almost as little about Evolution as he does about Transubstantiation. The Dean of St. Paul's does not, of course, put this truth in such plain words; but he manages to make it pretty plain. His candour in this case also has to be balanced by general expressions of agreement with the Bishop, and somewhat heartier expressions of disagreement with everybody else, especially with the Bishop's enemies. The Dean alludes scornfully to the orthodox world, as if it necessarily repudiated certain biological theories; or as if it mattered very much if it did. The difference between the Broad Churchman and the Catholic Church is not that the former thinks Evolution true and the latter thinks it false. It is that the former thinks Evolution an explanation and the latter knows it is not an explanation. Hence the former thinks it all important; and the latter thinks it rather unimportant. Being unable to grasp this principle, the Dean has to fall back on quoting an old Victorian cant phrase; and saying that a new scientific discovery passes through three stages: that of being called absurd; of being called anti-scriptural; and of being discovered to be quite old and familiar. He might have added that it generally goes on to a fourth stage; that of being discovered to be quite untrue.

For that is the very simple fact which both Dean Inge and Bishop Barnes leave out; and which seems to be as utterly unknown to the more lucid rationalism of the one as to the cruder secularism of the other. Not only was the Archbishop of Canterbury right in suggesting that old gentlemen like himself had been familiar with Evolution all their lives; but he might have added that they were much more certain of it in the earlier part of their lives than they will be by the end of their lives. Those of them who have really read the most recent European enquiries and speculations know that

Darwinism is every day becoming much less of a dogma and much more of a doubt. Those who have not read the speculations and the doubts simply go on repeating the dogma. While Dr. Barnes was preaching sermons carefully founded on the biology of fifty years ago, Mr. Belloc was proving conclusively before the whole world that Mr. H. G. Wells and Sir Arthur Keith were unacquainted with the biology of five years ago. In short, it is only just, as we have said, to insist on the difference between Dean Inge and Dr. Barnes; which is like the difference between Huxley and Haeckel. Everybody would be better and happier if Dean Inge were known as Professor Inge; and if Dr. Barnes were not only a Professor but a Prussian Professor. Then he could be boomed along with other barbarians attacking Christianity, without having the ecclesiastical privilege of actually persecuting Christians. But there are heathens and heathens and there are persecutors and persecutors. The Dean is a pagan Roman of the Senate House. The Bishop is a pagan Teuton of the swamps and fens. The Dean dislikes the Christian tradition in the spirit of Diocletian and Julian. The Bishop dislikes it in the simpler spirit of a Danish pirate staring at the rigid mystery of a Roman-British Church. Even the common cause and broad brotherly maxim of CHRISTIANI AD LEONES did not always, I fancy, reconcile the Roman and the Goth. These historical comparisons may seem fanciful; and indeed in one sense both parties are very much tied to their own historical period. They are both very Victorian; but even here there is a difference and a superiority. The superiority of the Dean is that he knows it and says so. He is man enough to boast of being Victorian and not to mind being called reactionary. Whereas the Bishop seems really to cherish the truly extraordinary notion that his notions are new and up-to-date.

Of course they have a philosophy in common; and it would be a cheap simplification to call it Materialism. Indeed, we should be almost as shallow in talking about Materialism as they are in talking about Magic. The truth is that the strange bigotry, which leads the Bishop to scream and rail at all sacramentalism as Magic, is in its inmost essence the very reverse of Materialism. Indeed it is nothing half so healthy as Materialism. The root of this prejudice is not so much a trust in matter as a sort of horror of matter. The man of this philosophy is always asking that worship shall be wholly spiritual, or even wholly intellectual; because he does really feel a disgust at the idea of spiritual things having a body and a solid form. It probably does really give him a mystical shudder to suppose that God can become as bread and wine; though I never understood why it should not give the same shudder to say that God could become flesh and blood. But whether or no these thinkers are logical in their philosophy, I think this is their philosophy. It has a very long history and an ancient name. It is not Materialist but Manichee.

Indeed the Dean uttered an unconscious truth when he said the sacramentalists must be "natural idolaters. " He shrinks from it not only because it is idolatrous, but also because it is natural. He cannot bear to think how natural is the craving for the supernatural. He cannot tolerate the idea of it actually working through the elements of nature. Unconsciously, no doubt, but very stubbornly, that sort of intellectual does feel that our souls may belong to God, but our bodies only to the devil or the beast. That Manichean horror of matter is the only INTELLIGENT reason for any such sweeping refusal of supernatural and sacramental wonders. The rest is all cant and repetition and arguing in a circle; all the baseless dogmatism about science forbidding men to believe in miracles; as if SCIENCE could forbid men to believe in something which science does not profess to investigate. Science is the study of the admitted laws of existence; it cannot prove a universal negative about whether those laws could ever be suspended by something admittedly above them. It is as if we were to say that a lawyer was so deeply learned in the American Constitution that he knew there could never be a revolution in America. Or it is as if a man were to say he was so close a student of the text of Hamlet that he was authorised to deny that an actor had dropped the skull and bolted when the theatre caught fire. The constitution follows a certain course, so long as it is there to follow it; the play follows a certain course, so long as it is being played; the visible order of nature follows a certain course if there is nothing behind it to stop it. But that fact throws no sort of light on whether there IS anything behind it to stop it. That is a question of philosophy or metaphysics and not of material science. And out of respect for the intelligence of both these reverend gentlemen, and especially for the high intelligence of the Dean of St. Paul's, I much prefer to think that they are opposed to what they call Magic as consistent philosophers and not as inconsistent scientists. I prefer to think that they are thinking along the lines of great Gnostics and Buddhists and other mystics of a dark but dignified historical tradition; rather than that they are blundering in plain logic in the interests of cheap popular science. I can even understand or imagine that thrill of repulsion that seizes them in the presence of the divine materialism of the Mass. But I still think they would be more consistent and complete, if they made it quite clear that they carried their principle to completion; and said, as the Moslem says about Christmas, "Far be it from Him to have a Son, " or the terrified disciples who cried, "Far be this from Thee, " when God was going up to be crucified.

WHAT WE THINK ABOUT

I WAS looking the other day at a weekly paper of the sort that is supposed to provide popular culture; in this case rather especially what may be called popular science. In practice it largely provides what its supporters optimistically call Modern Thought and what we more commonly call Modernism. It is, however, a paper by no means unfair or exclusive of the opposite point of view; it has more than once permitted me to reply to these views; and in looking at the issue in question, my eye was arrested by my own name.

It occurred in an article on the religious doctrines of Mr. Arnold Bennett. Indeed the prominence in the press of this name in this connection is one of the standing mysteries of modern journalism. I have not only a great admiration for the artistic genius, but in many ways a strong liking for the human personality of Mr. Arnold Bennett. I like his liveliness and contempt for contempt. I like his humanity and merciful curiosity about every thing human. I like that essential absence of snobbishness that enables him to sympathise even with snobs. But talking about the religious beliefs of Mr. Arnold Bennett seems to me exactly like talking about the foxhunting adventures of Mr. Bernard Shaw or the favourite vintages of Mr. Pussyfoot Johnson or the celestial visions of Sir Arthur Keith or the monastic vows of Mr. Bertrand Russell. Mr. Arnold Bennett has never disguised, as it seems to me, the essential fact that he has not got any religious beliefs; as religious beliefs were understood in the English language as I learnt it. That he has a number of highly estimable moral sentiments and sympathies I do not for a moment doubt. But the matter of Mr. Arnold Bennett is, for the moment, a parenthesis. I mention it here merely because it was in the course of such an article that I found myself mentioned; and I confess I thought the reference a little odd. It will not surprise the reader to learn that the writer found me less Modernist than Mr. Arnold Bennett. My religious beliefs did not present so pure and virgin and blameless a blank, but were defaced with definite statements about various things. But the writer professed to find something dubious or mysterious about my attitude; and what mystifies me is his mystification. He delicately implied that there was more in me than met the eye; that I had that within, which passed all these Papistical shows, but that it was hopeless to vivisect me and discover the secret. He said: "Mr. Chesterton does not mean to enlighten us; for all we know he is Modernist enough in his own thoughts. "

Now it would be thought a little annoying if an atheist were to say of some harmless Protestant Christian like General Booth; "For all we know, he is atheist enough in his own thoughts. " We might even venture to enquire how the atheist could possibly form any notion of what General Booth thought, in such complete contradiction to everything he said. Or I myself, on the other hand, might seem less than graceful, if I were to suggest that Mr. Arnold Bennett must be concealing his conversion out of cowardice; and were to express it in the form: "Mr. Bennett will never tell us the truth about it; for all we know he is Papist enough in his own thoughts. " I might even be cross-examined about how I had come to form these suspicions about the secret thoughts of Mr. Arnold Bennett; as to whether I had hidden under his bed and heard him muttering Latin prayers in his dreams, or sent a private detective to verify the existence of his hair-shirt and his concealed relics. It might be hinted that, until I could produce some such PRIMA FACIE case for my suspicions, it would be more polite to suppose that the opinions of Mr. Bennett were what he himself said they were. And if I were sensitive on such things, I might make a rather sharp request, that people who cannot possibly know anything about me except what I say, should for the sake of our general convenience believe what I say. On the subject of Modernism, at any rate, there has never been the least doubt or difficulty about what I say. For, as it happens, I had a strong intellectual contempt for Modernism, even before I really believed in Catholicism.

But I belong, as a biological product of evolution, to the order of the pachyderms. And I am not in the least moved by any annoyance in the matter; but only by a very strong mystification and curiosity about the real reason for this remarkable point of view. I know that the writer did not mean any harm; but I am much more interested in trying to understand what he did mean. And the truth is, I think, that there is hidden in this curious and cryptic phrase the secret of the whole modern controversy about Catholicism. What the man really meant was this: "Even poor old Chesterton must think; he can't have actually left off thinking altogether; there must be some form of cerebral function going forward to fill the empty hours of his misdirected and wasted life; and it is obvious that if a man begins to THINK, he can only think more or less in the direction of

Modernism. " The Modernists do really think that. That is the point. That is the joke.

Now what we have really got to hammer into the heads of all these people, somehow, is that a thinking man can think himself deeper and deeper into Catholicism, and not deeper and deeper into difficulties about Catholicism. We have got to make them see that conversion is the beginning of an active, fruitful, progressive and even adventurous life of the intellect. For THAT is the thing that they cannot at present bring themselves to believe. They honestly say to themselves: "What can he be thinking about, if he is not thinking about the Mistakes of Moses, as discovered by Mr. Miggles of Pudsey, or boldly defying all the terrors of the Inquisition which existed two hundred years ago in Spain? " We have got to explain somehow that the great mysteries like the Blessed Trinity or the Blessed Sacrament are the starting-points for trains of thought far more stimulating, subtle and even individual, compared with which all that sceptical scratching is as thin, shallow and dusty as a nasty piece of scandalmongering in a New England village. Thus, to accept the Logos as a truth is to be in the atmosphere of the absolute, not only with St. John the Evangelist, but with Plato and all the great mystics of the world. To accept the Logos as a "text" or an "interpolation" or a "development" or a dead word in a dead document, only used to give in rapid succession about six different dates to that document, is to be altogether on a lower plane of human life; to be squabbling and scratching for a merely negative success; even if it really were a success. To exalt the Mass is to enter into a magnificent world of metaphysical ideas, illuminating all the relations of matter and mind, of flesh and spirit, of the most impersonal abstractions as well as the most personal affections. To set out to belittle and minimise the Mass, by talking ephemeral back-chat about what it had in common with Mithras or the Mysteries, is to be in altogether a more petty and pedantic mood; not only lower than Catholicism but lower even than Mithraism.

As I have said before, it is very difficult to say how we can best set about these things. We and our critics have come to talk in two different languages; so that the very names by which we describe the things inside stand for totally different things in the absurd labels they have stuck upon the wall outside. Often if we said the great things we have to say, they would sound like the small things they accuse us of saying. A philosophical process can only begin at the right end; and they have got hold of everything by the wrong end.

But I am myself disposed to think that we should begin by challenging one very common phrase or form of words; a thing that has become a catch-word and a caption; or in the ordinary popular phrase a headline. Because the journalists incessantly repeat it, and draw attention to it by repeating it, we may possibly draw attention by denying it.

When the journalist says for the thousandth time, "Living religion is not in dull and dusty dogmas, etc. " we must stop him with a sort of shout and say, "There—you go wrong at the very start. " If he would condescend to ask what the dogmas are, he would find out that it is precisely the dogmas that are living, that are inspiring, that are intellectually interesting. Zeal and charity and unction are admirable as flowers and fruit; but if you are really interested in the living principle you must be interested in the root or the seed. In other words, you must be intelligently interested in the statement with which the whole thing started; even if it is only to deny it. Even if the critic cannot come to agree with the Catholic, he can come to see that it is certain ideas about the Cosmos that make him a Catholic. He can see that being Cosmic in that way, and Catholic in that way, is what makes him different from other people; and what makes him, at the very least, a not uninteresting figure in human history. He will never get anywhere near it by sentimentalising against Catholic sentiment or pontificating against Catholic pontiffs. He must get hold of the ideas as ideas; and he will find that the most interesting of all the ideas are those which the newspapers dismiss as dogmas.

For instance; the doctrine of the Dual Nature of Christ is in the most genuine sense interesting; it ought to be interesting to anybody who can understand it, long before he can believe it. It has what can be called with all reverence a stereoscopic interest; the interest of having the two eyes in the head that create an object; of having the two angles in the triangle that determine the third. The old Monophysite sect declared that Christ had only the one divine nature. The new Monophysite sect declares that He had only the one human nature. But it is not a pun or a trick, but a truth, to say that the Monophysite is by nature monotonous. In either of his two forms, he is naturally on one note. The question of objective historical truth is another question, which I am not arguing here, though I am ready to argue it anywhere. I am talking about intellectual stimulation and the starting point of thought and imagination. And these, like all living things, breed from the conjunction of two, and not from one alone. Thus I read, with sympathy but a sympathy that hardly goes beyond sentiment, the studies of the modern Monophysites in the life of the limited and merely mortal Jesus of Nazareth. I respect their respect; I admire their admiration; I know that all they say about human greatness or religious genius is true as far as it goes. But it goes along one line; and cannot convince like the things that can converge. And then, after reading such a tribute to an ethical teacher in the manner of the Essenes, perhaps I turn another page of the same or some similar book; and come upon some phrase used about a real though a pagan religion; perhaps some supposed parallel of what is called a Pagan Christ. I find it said, if only of Atys or Adonis, "There was a conception that the god sacrificed himself to himself. " The man who can read those words without a thrill is dead.

The thrill is deeper for us, of course, because it is concerned with a fact and not a fancy. In that sense we do not admit that there is any such parallel with the legends of the ancient pagans as is implied in the books of the modern pagans. And indeed we are surely entitled to call it mere common sense to say that there can be no complete parallel between what was admittedly a myth or mystery and what was admittedly a man. But the point here is that the truth hidden even in myths and mysteries is altogether lost if we are confined to the consideration of a man. In this sense there is an ironic and unconscious truth in the words of the modern pagan, who sang that "the heathen outface and outlive us, " and that "our lives and our longings are twain. " It is true of the Modernists, but it is not true of us, who find simultaneously the realisation of a longing and the record of a life. It is perfectly true that there were in many pagan myths the faint foreshadowing of the Christian mysteries; though even in saying so we admit that the foreshadowings were shadows. But when all imaginative kinship has been explored or allowed for, it is not true that mythology ever rose to the heights of theology. It is not true that a thought so bold or so subtle as this one ever crossed the mind that created the centaurs and the fauns. In the wildest and most gigantic of the primitive epic fancies, there is no conception so colossal as the being who is both Zeus and Prometheus.

But I only advert to it here, not as arguing its truth against those who do not believe it, but only as insisting on its intense and intellectual interest for those who do believe it. I only wish to explain to those who are worried in this way, that a mind filled with the true conception of this Duality has plenty to think about along those lines and has no need to dig up dead gods to discredit the Everlasting

Man. There is no necessity for me to be Modernist in my own thoughts, or Monophysite in my own thoughts; because I think these views much duller and more trivial than my own. In the beautiful words of the love-song in THE WALLET OF KAI LUNG, one of the few truly psychological love-songs of the world: "This insignificant and universally despised person would unhesitatingly prefer his thoughts to theirs. "

Any number of other examples could of course be given. This person (if I may use once more the graceful Chinese locution) would very soon exhaust the excitement of discovering that Mary and Maia both begin with an M, or that the Mother of Christ and the Mother of Cupid were both represented as women. But I know that I shall never exhaust the profundity of that unfathomable paradox which is defined so defiantly in the very title of the Mother of God. I know that there are not only far deeper, but far fresher and freer developments of thought and imagination, in that riddle of the perfectly human having once had a natural authority over the supernaturally divine, than in any sort of iconoclastic identification which assimilates all the sacred images by flattening all their faces. By the time that Christ is really made the same as Osiris, there can be very little left of either of them; but Christ, as conceived by the Catholic Church, is himself a complex and a combination, not of two unreal things, but of two real ones. In the same way an Ashtaroth exactly like one of Raphael's Madonnas, or vice versa, would seem a somewhat featureless vision in any case; whereas there is something that is, in the most intellectual sense, unique about the conception of the THEOTOKOS. In short, in all this mere unification of traditions, true or false, there is something that may be quite simply described as dull. But the dogmas are not dull. Even what are called the fine doctrinal distinctions are not dull. They are like the finest operations of surgery; separating nerve from nerve, but giving life. It is easy enough to flatten out everything for miles round with dynamite, if our only object is to give death. But just as the physiologist is dealing with living tissues, so the theologian is dealing with living ideas; and if he draws a line between them it is naturally a very fine line. It is the custom, though by this time; already a rather stale custom, to complain that the Greeks or Italians who disputed about the Trinity or the Sacrament were splitting hairs. I do not know that even splitting hairs is any drearier than bleaching hairs, in the vain attempt to match the golden hair of Freya and the black hair of Cotytto. The subdivision of a hair does at least tell us something of its structure; whereas its mere discoloration tells us nothing at all.

Theology does introduce us to the structure of ideas; whereas theosophical syncretism merely washes all the colours out of the coloured fairy-tales of the world. But my only purpose in this place is to reassure the kind gentleman who was troubled about the secret malady of modernity that must be eating away my otherwise empty mind. I hasten earnestly to explain that I am quite well, thank you; and that I have plenty of things to think about without falling back on a Baconian madness of pagan parallels, or establishing the connection between the tale of the bull killed by Mithras and the tune the old cow died of.

THE OPTIMIST AS A SUICIDE

FREETHINKERS are occasionally thoughtful, though never free. In the modern world of the West, at any rate, they seem always to be tied to the treadmill of a materialist and monist cosmos. The universal sceptic, in Asia or in Antiquity, has probably been a bolder thinker, though very probably a more unhappy man. But what we have to deal with as scepticism is not scepticism; but a fixed faith in monism. The freethinker is not free to question monism. He is forbidden, for instance, in the only intelligible modern sense, to believe in a miracle. He is forbidden, in exactly the same sense in which he would say that we are forbidden to believe in a heresy. Both are forbidden by first principles and not by force. The Rationalist Press Association will not actually kidnap, gag or strangle Sir Arthur Keith if he admits the evidence for a cure at Lourdes. Neither will the Cardinal Archbishop of Westminster have me hanged, drawn and quartered if I announce that I am an agnostic tomorrow. But of both cases it is true to say that a man cannot root up his first principles without a terrible rending and revolutionising of his very self. As a matter of fact, we are the freer of the two; as there is scarcely any evidence, natural or preternatural, that cannot be accepted as fitting into our system somewhere; whereas the materialist cannot fit the most minute miracle into his system anywhere. But let us leave that on one side as a separate question; and agree, if only for the sake of argument, that both the Catholic and the materialist are limited only by their fundamental conviction about the cosmic system; in both thought is in that sense forbidden and in that sense free. Consequently, when I see in some newspaper symposium, like that on Spiritualism, a leading materialist like Mr. John M. Robertson discussing the evidence for spiritualism, I feel exactly as I imagine him to feel when he hears a bishop in a mitre or a Jesuit in a cassock discussing the evidence for materialism. I know that Mr. Robertson cannot accept the evidence without becoming somebody quite different from Mr. Robertson; which also is within the power of the grace of God. But I know quite well he is not a freethinker; except in the sense in which I am a freethinker. He has long ago come to a conclusion which controls all his other conclusions. He is not driven by scientific evidence to accept Materialism. He is forbidden by Materialism to accept scientific evidence.

But there is another way in which the freethinker is not only thoughtful, but useful. The man who rejects the Faith altogether is often very valuable as a critic of the man who rejects it piecemeal, or bit by bit, or by fits and starts. The man who picks out some part of Catholicism that happens to please him, or throws away some part that happens to puzzle him, does in fact produce, not only the queerest sort of result, but generally the very opposite result to what he intends. And his inconsistency can often be effectively exposed from the extreme negative as well as the extreme positive point of view. It has been said that when the half-gods go, the gods arrive; it might be said in amiable parody that when the no-goddites arrive, the half-goddites go; and I am not sure it is not a good riddance. Anyhow, even the atheist can illustrate how important it is to keep the Catholic system altogether, even if he rejects it altogether.

A curious and amusing instance comes from America; in connection with Mr. Clarence Darrow, the somewhat simple-minded sceptic of that land of simplicity. He seems to have been writing something about the impossibility of anybody having a soul; of which nothing need be said except that (as usual) it seems to be the sceptic who really thinks of the soul superstitiously, as a separate and secret animal with wings; who considers the soul quite apart from the self. But what interests me about him at the moment is this. One of his arguments against immortality is that people do not really believe in it. And one of his arguments for that is that if they did believe in certain happiness beyond the grave, they would all kill themselves. He says that nobody would endure the martyrdom of cancer, for instance, if he really believed (as he apparently assumes all Christians to believe) that in any case the mere fact of death would instantly introduce the soul to perfect felicity and the society of all its best friends. A Catholic will certainly know what answer he has to give. But Mr. Clarence Darrow does not really in the least know what question he has asked.

Now there we have the final flower and crown of all modern optimism and universalism and humanitarianism in religion. Sentimentalists talk about love till the world is sick of the most glorious of all human words; they assume that there can be nothing in the next world except the sort of Utopia of practical pleasure which they promise us (but do not give us) in this world. They declare that all will be forgiven, because there is nothing to forgive. They insist that "passing over" is only like going into the next room, they insist that it will not even be a waiting-room. They declare that it must immediately introduce us to a cushioned lounge with all conceivable comforts, without any reference to how we have got there. They are positive that there is no danger, no devil; even no death. All is hope, happiness and optimism. And, as the atheist very truly points out, the logical result of all that hope, happiness and optimism would be hundreds of people hanging from lamp-posts or thousands of people throwing themselves into wells or canals. We should find the rational result of the modern Religion of Joy and Love in one huge human stampede of suicide. Pessimism would have killed its thousands, but optimism its ten thousands.

Now, of course, as I say, a Catholic knows the answer; because he holds the complete philosophy, which keeps a man sane; and not some single fragment of it, whether sad or glad, which may easily drive him mad. A Catholic does not kill himself because he does not take it for granted that he will deserve heaven in any case, or that it will not matter at all whether he deserves it at all. He does not profess to know exactly what danger he would run; but he does know what loyalty he would violate and what command or condition he would disregard. He actually thinks that a man might be fitter for heaven because he endured like a man; and that a hero could be a martyr to cancer as St. Lawrence or St. Cecilia were martyrs to cauldrons or gridirons. The faith in a future life, the hope of a future happiness, the belief that God is Love and that loyalty is eternal life, these things do not produce lunacy and anarchy, IF they are taken along with the other Catholic doctrines about duty and vigilance and watchfulness against the powers of hell. They might produce lunacy and anarchy, if they were taken alone. And the Modernists, that is, the optimists and the sentimentalists, did want us to take them alone. Of course, the same would be true, if somebody took the other doctrines of duty and discipline alone. It would produce another dark age of Puritans rapidly blackening into Pessimists. Indeed, the extremes meet, when they are both ends clipped off what should be a complete thing. Our parable ends poetically with two gibbets side by side; one for the suicidal pessimist and the other for the suicidal optimist.

The point is that in this passage the American sceptic is answering the Modernist; but he is not answering the Catholic. The Catholic has an extremely simple and sensible reason for not cutting his throat in order to fly instantly into Paradise. But he might really raise a question for those who talk as if Paradise were invariably and instantly populated with people who had cut their throats. And this is only one example out of a long list of historical examples; in which those who tried to make the Faith more simple invariably made it less sane. The Moslems imagined that they were merely being sensible when they cut down the creed to a mere belief in one God; but in the world of practical psychology they really cut it down to one Fate. The actual effect on ordinary men was simply fatalism; like that of the Turk who will not take his wound to a hospital because he is resigned to Kismet or the will of Allah. The Puritans thought they were simplifying things by appealing to what they called the plain words of Scripture; but as a fact they were complicating things by bringing in half a hundred cranky sects and crazy suggestions. And the modern universalist and humanitarian thought they were simplifying things when they interpreted the great truth that God is Love, as meaning that there can be no war with the demons or no danger to the soul. But in fact they were inventing even darker riddles with even wilder answers; and Mr. Clarence Darrow has suggested one of them. He will be gratified to receive the thanks of all Catholics for doing so.

THE OUTLINE OF THE FALL

I HAVE remarked on the curious rearguard action of bluff that is being fought to cover the retreat of the Darwinians. An example of the same thing has appeared in connection with a much more famous name; indeed, with two famous names. Mr. H. G. Wells has replied to Mr. Belloc, who wrote a criticism of the "Outline of History, " chiefly to protest against a certain tone of arbitrary generalisation and sham knowledge of the unknown. A typical case was that in which Mr. Wells said of the men who drew reindeers in caves: "There seems no scope in such a life for speculation or philosophy, " and Mr. Belloc not unnaturally answered: "Why on earth not? " But the details of the various works in question do not concern me immediately here; they mostly depend on that habit of talking as if every cave-drawing had its date obligingly inscribed on it; or any stone hatchet might bear the inscription 400,000 B. C. or possibly, B.O. H., or Before the Outline of History. At the moment the only point of contact is that which affects a continuation of our previous criticism, touching the present state of Darwinism. And what strikes me is that even Mr. Wells, often a sufficiently warm controversialist, is relatively and really cold in the matter; and his defence of Darwin is much more of an apology than an apologia. Indeed, like so many other modern apologies, it almost amounts to pleading that Darwin was not a Darwinian.

The Victorian evolutionists devoted themselves to declaring how great Darwin's thesis was. The new evolutionists seem to devote themselves to explaining how small it was. They really seem to plead, as in the old anecdote, that it gave birth to a theory, but a very little one. Some of Mr. Wells's words may surely, without unfairness, be called apologetic. He does not, like the professor previously mentioned, try to get over the word "origin" by talking about "the cause of the origin. " So he concentrates on the word "species, " as if evolution had not only applied to a sub-division. He adds that Darwin did not at the beginning even apply it to man. What in the world would the Victorian Darwinians have said had they heard it urged in defence of Darwinism that it was not applied to man? Are we to understand that only the first book of Darwin is divinely inspired? Again, Mr. Wells says that natural selection is common sense. And doubtless, if it only means that things fitted for survival do survive, it is common sense. We may also add that it is common knowledge. Has it come to this, that Darwin is defended because he only discovered what was common knowledge? The real question, of course, is that stated by Mr. Belloc; when he said that nobody needs to be told that in a flood fish live and cattle die. The question is, How soon do cattle turn into fish? That would be an example of the true Darwinian theory; and it is now merely minimised, represented as only one element of evolution and without even the elements of an explanation. We fancy there is a healthy prejudice behind it all. Mr. Wells indignantly repudiates the slander uttered by Mr. Belloc, who called him a patriot. But it is true; the deep English national pride has much to do with this devotion. And rather than deprive England of her Darwin, they have deprived Darwin of his discovery.

When a man is as great a genius as Mr. Wells, I admit it sounds provocative to call him provincial. But if he wants to know why anybody does it, it will be enough to point silently to the headline of one of his pages, which runs: "Where is the Garden of Eden? " To come down to a thing like that, and to think it telling, when talking to an intelligent Catholic about the Fall, that IS provinciality; proud and priceless provinciality. The French peasants of whom Mr. Wells speaks are not in that sense provincial. As Mr. Wells says, they do not know anything about Darwin and Evolution. They do not know and they do not care. That is where they are much better philosophers than Mr. Wells. They hold the philosophy of the Fall, in the form of a simple story which may be historic or symbolic, but anyhow cannot be more important than what it symbolises. In comparison with that truth, it does not matter twopence whether any evolutionary theory is true or not. Whether or no the garden was an allegory, the truth itself can be very well allegorised as a garden. And the point of it is that Man, whatever else he is, is certainly NOT merely one of the plants of the garden that has plucked its roots out of the soil and walked about with them like legs, or on the principle of a double dahlia has grown duplicate eyes and ears. He is something else, something strange and solitary; and more like the statue that was once the god of the garden; but the statue has fallen from its pedestal and lies broken among the plants and weeds. This conception has nothing to do with materialism as it refers to materials. The image might be made of wood; the wood might have come from the garden; the sculptor presumably might, and probably did, allow for the growth and grain of the wood in what he carved and expressed. But my fable fixes the two truths of the true scripture. The first is that the wood was graven or stamped with an image, deliberately, and from the outside; in this case the image of God. The second is that this image has been damaged and defaced, so that it is now both better and worse than the mere plants in the garden, which are perfect according to their own plan. There is room for any amount of speculation about the history of the tree before it was turned into an image; there is room for any amount of doubt and mystery about what really happened when it was turned into an image; there is room for any amount of hope and imagination about what it will look like when it is really mended and made into the perfect statue we have never seen. But it has the two fixed points, that man was uplifted at the first and fell; and to answer it by saying, "Where is the Garden of Eden? " is like answering a philosophical Buddhist by saying, "When were you last a donkey? "

The Fall is a view of life. It is not only the only enlightening, but the only encouraging view of life. It holds, as against the only real alternative philosophies, those of the Buddhist or the Pessimist or the Promethean, that we have misused a good world, and not merely been entrapped into a bad one. It refers evil back to the wrong use of the will, and thus declares that it can eventually be righted by the right use of the will. Every other creed except that one is some form of surrender to fate. A man who holds this view of life will find it giving light on a thousand things; on which mere evolutionary ethics have not a word to say. For instance, on the colossal contrast between the completeness of man's machines and the continued corruption of his motives; on the fact that no social progress really seems to leave self behind; on the fact that the first and not the last men of any school or revolution are generally the best and purest; as William Penn was better than a Quaker millionaire or Washington better than an American oil magnate; on that proverb that says: "The price of liberty is eternal vigilance, " which is only what the theologians say of every other virtue, and is itself only a way of stating the truth of original sin; on those extremes of good and evil by which man exceeds all the animals by the measure of heaven and hell; on that sublime sense of loss that is in the very sound of all great poetry, and nowhere more than in the poetry of pagans and sceptics: "We look before and after, and pine for what is not"; which cries against all prigs and progressives out of the very depths and abysses of the broken heart of man, that happiness is not only a hope, but also in some strange manner a memory; and that we are all kings in exile.

Now to people who feel that this view of life is more real, more radical, more universal than the cheap simplifications opposed to it, it comes with quite a shock of bathos to realise that anybody let alone a man like Mr. Wells, supposes that it all depends on some detail about the site of a garden in Mesopotamia, like that identified by General Gordon. It is hard to find any parallel to such an incongruity; for there is no real similarity between our muddled mortal affairs and events that were divine if they were mysterious, and scriptures that are sacred even if they are symbolical. But some shadow of a comparison could be made out of the modern myths. I mean the sort of myths that men like Mr. Wells generally do believe in; such as the Myth of Magna Carta or the Myth of the Mayflower. Now many historians will maintain that Magna Carta was really nothing to speak of; that it was largely a piece of feudal privilege. But suppose one of the historians who holds this view began to argue with us excitedly about the fabulous nature of our ordinary fancy picture of Magna Carta. Suppose he produced maps and documents to prove that Magna Carta was not signed at Runnymede, but somewhere else; as I believe some scholars do maintain. Suppose he criticised the false heraldry and fancy-dress costumes of the ordinary sort of waxwork historical picture of the event. We should think he was rather unduly excited about a detail of mediaeval history. But with what a shock of astonishment should we realise at last that the man actually thought that all modern attempts at democracy must be abandoned, that all representative government must be wrong, that all Parliaments would have to be dissolved and all political rights destroyed, if once it were admitted that King John did not sign that special document in that little island in the Thames! What should we think of him, if he really thought we had no reasons for liking law or liberty, except the authenticity of that beloved royal signature? That is very much how I feel when I find that Mr. Wells really imagines that the luminous and profound philosophy of the Fall only means that Eden was somewhere in Mesopotamia. Now the only explanation of a great man like Mr. Wells having a small prejudice, like this about the snake, is that he does come of a religious tradition that regarded the text of Hebrew Scripture as the only authority and had forgotten all about the great mediaeval metaphysic and the discussion of fundamental ideas. The man who does that is provincial; and there is no harm in saying so even when he is one of the greatest men of letters and a glory to the English name.

THE IDOLS OF SCOTLAND

THE thing that strikes me most in current controversy is that our opponents are talking almost entirely in terms of the past, and that an entirely dead past; whereas we are making some sort of attempt, whether it be considered impertinent or eccentric or meddlesome or paradoxical, to deal with the practical conditions of the present. An amusing comedy on these lines seems to have arisen on the subject of Scottish Nationalism or the notion of Home Rule for North Britain. A worthy Presbyterian has warned his fellow-countrymen that the movement is tainted by the presence of Roman Catholics, and especially by that of Mr. Compton Mackenzie; and that no little degree of the deadly peril is indicated by the fact that Mr. Cunninghame Graham is interested in a book by Mr. Belloc; in which the hideous sentiment is uttered that the Reformation was the shipwreck of Christendom. Personally I should have thought it was obvious to anybody on any side, in one solid and objective sense, that it was the shipwreck of Christendom. I should imagine that it would be obvious to anybody, for instance, who desires or even discusses the Reunion of Christendom. There certainly was a united vessel or vehicle and it certainly did break up into different parts. Some people may think the ship was a rotten old-fashioned three-decker that was bound to break up; and that the people were lucky who got away from it in boats. But it is certain that it did break up and that the boats were not the same as the original ship. A man might as well resent our saying that the rise of the feudal kingdoms and the modern nationalities was part of the decline and fall of the Roman Empire. This is only one of the marks of such bigotry; but it is worth noting at the outset. One of the peculiarities of this sort of bigot is that he cannot distinguish between provocative statements and plain inevitable statements. If I say that the Reformation was a relapse into barbarism, a return to all that was worst in the Dark Ages without anything of what was best in them, an idolatry of dead Hebrew documents full of visions and symbols without any Daniel to interpret the dreams, a stampede of brutal luxury and pride with a vulgar howl of hot-gospelling for an excuse, a riot of thieves and looters with a few foaming and gibbering lunatics carried in front of it like live mascots for luck; the return of the Manichee, the dirty ape of the ascetic, conspiring with the devil to destroy the world— if I were to say all this I should think that these remarks about Protestantism certainly had a slightly provocative flavour. But if I were to say, with Mr. Belloc, that Protestantism was the shipwreck of

Christendom, I should regard it as an ordinary historical statement, like saying that the American War of Independence was a split in the British Empire. The bigot cannot see the difference between these two types of statement, whether made by us or by himself.

The next interesting thing to note about the protest is that the Protestant goes on to say that Mr. Compton Mackenzie and his friends are going to ruin Scotland by removing the stern teaching of John Knox, which has apparently created the Scottish character. This seems a little hard on the Scottish character. I cannot quite bring myself to believe that the character of Scott or of Stevenson, the character of Burns or Barrie, are exact and unaltered reproductions of the stern teaching of John Knox. But before we come to any such comparisons, it is worth remarking, on the face of the thing that a rather more living world, a life more in touch with modern conditions, a grasp of the actual problems of the present and the immediate future, is rather more indicated by saying the words "Compton Mackenzie" than by saying the words "John Knox. " Many very modern young men have recently joined the same religion as Mr. Compton Mackenzie. No such modern young men, that I ever heard of, have ever exhibited the smallest desire to go back to the religion of John Knox. As a matter of plain fact, there is hardly one modern Scotsman in a thousand who has the smallest sympathy with the real religion of John Knox. He may vaguely respect John Knox as a Scottish hero, on the supposition (quite startlingly false) that he was a Scottish patriot. As a matter of fact, the patriotic party in Scotland was the wicked Papistical party; Knox and his Presbyterians were all for helping the pressure of England and Elizabeth. They would have justified themselves by saying that they had the one, true and only right religion. The question is, who is left even in Scotland who believes that it was the one, true and only right religion? I repeat, about one in a thousand; perhaps only a few splendidly fanatical old Wee Frees in the Highlands. Anybody who knows anything of the Scottish Presbyterian Churches, during the last fifty years, knows that the prevailing doctrine taught in them has NOT been the severe Calvinism of the eighteenth and seventeenth centuries, still less the wild Calvinism of the sixteenth. It has been a mild hash of Hegelian philosophy and Higher Criticism, all borrowed from Germany and carefully learnt by Scotch students in German Universities. And anybody who has noticed what the modern Scottish character is really like, knows that it does not by this time (thank heaven) bear the smallest resemblance to the sternness of John Knox. It is rather sentimental than otherwise, though its sentiment finds expression in more than one brilliant and admirable man of genius. Modern Scotland is not even remotely represented by John Knox. It is represented much more accurately, and much more honourably, by Sir Harry Lauder and Sir James Barrie.

This dull habit of invoking dead things, in a world in which we are surrounded by more and more interesting living things, is the second mark of the sort of bigot I am describing. It would be an extremely interesting business to write a real, respectful and sympathetic history of the remarkable episode of Scottish Puritanism; insisting on its integrity and its intellectual vigour while it lasted. But any sincere study of it must conclude with the statement that it did not last. One of the most brilliant and distinguished of Scottish professors, at Edinburgh University, himself of an origin wholly Puritan and of sympathies the very reverse of Catholic, used to me the true and forcible expression about the old Scottish Sabbatarianism, "It covered all Scotland; and then one morning, it had suddenly vanished everywhere like the snow. " And though the story might be told truly from either standpoint, or from many others, it is but natural that we should draw our own moral from it. And the moral is, of course, one which we find running through the whole of our history.

The birth and death of every heresy has been essentially the same. A morbid or unbalanced Catholic takes one idea out of the thousandfold throng of Catholic ideas; and announces that he cares for that Catholic idea more than for Catholicism. He takes it away with him into a wilderness, where the idea becomes an image and the image an idol. Then, after a century or two, he suddenly wakes up and discovers that the idol is an idol; and, shortly after that, that the wilderness is a wilderness. If he is a wise man, he calls himself a fool. If he is a fool, he calls himself an evolutionary progressive who has outgrown the worship of idols; and he looks round him at the wilderness, spreading bare and desolate on every side and says, in the beautiful words of Mr. H. G. Wells: "I see no limit to it at all. "

That is what happened to the Calvinistic Scotsman; and the chief comfort in the prospect is that the Scotsman is not generally a fool, even when he has ceased to be a Calvinist. But he very often becomes an atheist; and the fact that so many of the hard destructive sceptics, from Hume downwards, came from Scotland, was the early and significant evidence of the discovery of the idol and the wilderness. But in any case, that is the compact parable of what occurred. The Calvinist was a Catholic whose imagination had been in some way caught and overpowered by the one isolated theological truth of the power and knowledge of God; and he offered to it human sacrifice, not only of every human sentiment, but of every other divine quality. Something in that bare idea of all-seeing, all-searching and pitiless power intoxicated and exalted certain men for a certain period, as certain men are intoxicated by a storm of wind or some terrible stage tragedy. The more moderate Protestants, the Anglicans and to a large extent the Lutherans, had something of the same queer feeling about the King. Hence came the Cavalier doctrine of Divine Right—and the court chaplains of Prussia. Nothing is more intriguing and challenging to the imagination than the necessity of trying to understand how men in the sixteenth and early seventeenth centuries felt a sort of abstract altruistic joy in the mere might and triumph of the Prince; in the mere autocracy of the earthly ruler. The Calvinists, to do them justice, felt it only about the heavenly ruler. In that sense the Scots can look proudly back on their Calvinism. But they cannot look proudly forward to Calvinism. They really know, as well as anybody else, that this isolated religious idea can no longer be kept separate from all the other religious ideas to which it belongs. The Calvinism of the Puritan is as dead as the Divine Right of the Cavaliers; men can no longer worship the idol, whether it is Presbyterianism or Erastianism. They can only worship the wilderness; which is atheism—or, as the more polite say, pantheism.

Whether it be called a Catholic tendency or no, all the movements of all the sects of late have been in the direction of trying to put together again those separate pieces that were pulled apart in the sixteenth century. The main feature of our time has been the fact that one person after another has recovered one piece after another, and added it to the new scheme by borrowing it from the old. There is one sufficient proof that there has indeed been a shipwreck. And that is that Robinson Crusoe has, ever since, been continually going back to get things from the wreck.

IF THEY HAD BELIEVED

ONE of the things our enemies do not know is the real case for their own side. It is always for me a great matter of pride that the proudest, the most genuine and the most unanswerable boast, that the Protestants of England could ever make, was made for them by a Catholic. Very few of the Protestants, of his time at any rate, would have had the historical enlargement or enlightenment to make it. For it was said by Newman, when that great master of English was surveying the glorious triumphs of our tongue from Bacon and Milton, to Swift and Burke, and he reminded us firmly that, though we convert England to the true faith a thousand times over, "English literature will always HAVE BEEN Protestant. "

That generous piece of candour might well be represented as even too generous; but I think it is very wise for us to be too generous. It is not entirely, or at least not exclusively true. The name of Chaucer is alone enough to show that English literature was English a long time before it was Protestant. Even a Protestant, if he were also English, could ask for nobody more entirely English than Chaucer. He was, in the essential national temper, very much more English than Milton. As a matter of fact, the argument is no stronger for Chaucer than it is for Shakespeare. But in the case of Shakespeare the argument is long and complicated, as conducted by partisans; though sufficiently simple and direct for people with a sense of reality. I believe that recent discoveries, as recorded in a book by a French lady, have very strongly confirmed the theory that Shakespeare died a Catholic. But I need no books and no discoveries to prove to me that he had lived a Catholic, or more probably, like the rest of us, tried unsuccessfully to live a Catholic; that he thought like a Catholic and felt like a Catholic and saw every question as a Catholic sees it. The proofs of this would be matter for a separate essay; if indeed so practical an impression can be proved at all. It is quite self-evident to me that he was a certain real and recognisable Renaissance type of Catholic; like Cervantes; like Ronsard. But if I were asked offhand for a short explanation, I could only say that I know he was a Catholic from the passages which are now used to prove he was an agnostic.

But that is another and much more subtle question, which is not the question I proposed to myself in starting this essay. In starting it, I proposed to grant the whole sound and solid truth of Newman's admission; that there has indeed arisen out of the disunion of Europe a great and glorious English Protestant literature; and to make some further speculations upon the point. And I think that nothing could make clearer to the modern English, the one supreme thing that they don't know (which is what our religion really is and why we think it real) than to put this rather interesting historical question. What difference would it have made to the great masters of English literature, if they had been Catholics?

Of course, the question cannot be strictly and scientifically answered; because nobody knows what difference would be made to anybody by any change in the circumstances of his life. But taking the matter broadly, as a question of ideas or even of doctrines it is worth asking as a matter of religious history. How far did the great Protestant writers depend on Protestantism?

I have no intention of discussing it adequately here; and indeed this is not so much an essay as an essay to suggest an essay. It is, in fact, a delicate indication, to people more learned than myself, that I am in possession of a very good title and subject for an essay. But at least it will be safe to say that the common or conventional impression among English people on this point is wildly wrong. It is wrong because it imagines that purely Protestant ideas were in some vague way the same as liberal and emancipated ideas. And it is wrong in a more special sense, because it is founded on the utterly false history, which supposes that the Renaissance was the same as the Reformation. It would be very difficult to say what English literature owes to the Reformation as distinct from the Renaissance. There is the splendid sincerity that inspired the plain English of Bunyan; but even Bunyan was a sort of exception that proved the rule. He was a Puritan; but he was emphatically not a Puritan of the Puritans. He was a man actually suspected by his fellow Puritans, because he was not so much a Puritan as a Christian. It was remarked at the time, and it has often been remarked since, that his theory is not very sectarian by the standard of seventeenth century sects. Among the Calvinists he was so much of a moderate, that thousands must have read his great book without thinking about Calvinism at all. And if we take the great scenes in his great book, the battle with Apollyon, the Mission of Greatheart, the death of Valiant-for-the-Truth, when all the trumpets sounded on the other side—there is really no reason whatever why they should not have been written by a Catholic. I do not affirm that they WOULD have been written by a Catholic, if the course of history had left the common people Catholics; for that is a question which nobody can possibly answer one way or the other.

But I am speaking strictly of doctrines in their relation to ideas and images; and there is no possible reason why a Catholic should be prevented by his Catholicism from writing such a story of the pilgrimage of Man and the fight to attain to God.

Milton in one way is an even stronger case; since he had much more in him of Shakespeare and the Catholic Renaissance. And I really cannot think of any deep difference that it would have made to his poetry, as poetry, if he had followed other members of his family in the old faith; I do not see that he need have been much altered, except possibly by being a much jollier man. Many will not realise this, because they insist on regarding artistic and intellectual freedom as something that was closed to the Catholic countries and open only to the Protestant. But all history is in flat contradiction to this view. The tide of culture in the seventeenth century flowed from France to England, not from England to France. Milton might have been as central as Moliere and still remained a Catholic man in a Catholic atmosphere. Descartes the Catholic was more truly than Bacon the Protestant, the PHILOSOPHER of rationalist science. The experiments, the new forms, the great names in criticism and philosophy, appeared during the last two or three centuries quite as much in the Catholic countries as in the Protestant, if not rather more. England could have produced a great English literature, as France produced a great French literature, without any change in the ancient European religion.

The real test case, to be considered in some such essay, would be a case like that of Cowper. There you do most emphatically have the Protestant theology; and there you do most emphatically have the English poetry. But the two have precious little to do with each other; until the coming of that dark hour when the theology destroyed the poetry. Poor Cowper's Calvinism drove him mad; and only his poetry managed for some time to keep him sane. But there was nothing whatever either in the poetry or the sanity that could have prevented him from being a Catholic. On the contrary, he was exactly the sort of man who would have been very happy as a Catholic. He was the sort of man to have been devoted to the memory of St. Francis, if he had ever heard of him; and there was nothing to prevent the one any more than the other from keeping pet birds or stroking wild hares out of the woods. It was the brutal blow of Calvin, two centuries before, that broke the heart of that natural saint; and it is not the least of his crimes.

After the time of Cowper, there does indeed begin to appear another type of difficulty; but it is not the presence but rather the absence of Protestant theology. There were elements even in Burns and Byron, there were still more elements in Shelley and Swinburne, which would doubtless have been at issue with their Catholic tradition, if they had had it. But it would not have been a revolt against Catholicism half so much as it was a revolt against Protestantism. In so far as they tended to mere scepticism, they could have found their way to it more quickly from reading Rabelais and Montaigne in a Catholic country than from reading Shakespeare and Milton in a Protestant one. As soon as the Revolution has begun, in a sense as soon as the Romantic Movement has begun, the positive Puritan theology is left behind even more completely than the mediaeval theology. Indeed the Romantics did develop a faint and hazy sympathy, if not with mediaeval theology, at least with mediaeval religion. It is true that Byron or Hugo probably preferred an abbey to be a ruined abbey; but they would not have visited a Baptist chapel even for the pleasure of seeing it ruined. It is true that Scott advised us to see mediaeval Melrose by moonlight; with the delicate implication that the mediaeval religion was moonshine. But he would not in any case have wanted to see Exeter Hall by gaslight; and he would have thought its theology not moonshine but gas. The tributes which he occasionally forces himself to make to the official Puritanism of his own country are, it will be generally agreed, the most sullen and insincere words to be found in his works. On the negative side, therefore, the conclusion is altogether negative. It is very difficult to find, at least after the doubtful case of Bunyan and the deadly case of Cowper, anything that can be called a purely literary inspiration coming from the purely Protestant doctrines. There is plenty of inspiration coming more or less indirectly from Paganism; but after the first excitement, hardly any from Protestantism.

If this is true on the negative side, it is even truer on the positive side. I take it that the imaginative magnificence of Milton's epic, in such matters as the War in Heaven, would have been much more convincing, if it had been modelled more on the profound mediaeval mysteries about the nature of angels and archangels, and less on the merely fanciful Greek myths about giants and gods. PARADISE LOST is an immortal poem; but it has just failed to be an immortal religious poem. Those are most happy in reading Milton who can read him as they would read Hesiod. It is doubtful whether those seeking spiritual satisfaction now read him even as naturally as they would read Crashaw. I suppose nobody will dispute that the pageantry of Scott might have taken on a tenfold splendour if he could have understood the emblems of an everlasting faith as sympathetically as he did the emblems of a dead feudalism. For him it was the habit that made the monk; but the habit would have been quite as picturesque if there had been a real monk inside it; let alone a real mind inside the monk, like the mind of St. Dominic or St. Hugh of Lincoln. "English literature will always have been Protestant"; but it might have been Catholic; without ceasing to be English literature, and perhaps succeeding in producing a deeper literature and a happier England.

PEACE AND THE PAPACY

THERE is a famous saying which to some has seemed lacking in reverence, though in fact it is a support of one important part of religion; "If God had not existed, it would have been necessary to invent Him. " It is not at all unlike some of the daring questions with which St. Thomas Aquinas begins his great defence of the faith. Some of the modern critics of his faith, especially the Protestant critics of it, have fallen into an amusing error, chiefly through ignorance of Latin and of the old use of the word DIVUS, and have accused Catholics of describing the Pope as God. Catholics, I need not say, are about as likely to call the Pope God as to call a grasshopper the Pope. But there is a sense in which they do recognise an eternal correspondence between the position of the King of Kings in the universe and of his Viceroy in the world, like the correspondence between a real thing and its shadow; a similarity something like the damaged and defective similarity between God and the image of God. And among the coincidences of this comparison may be classed the case of this epigram. The world will more and more find itself in a position in which even politicians and practical men will find themselves saying, "If the Pope had not existed, it would be necessary to invent him. "

It is not at all impossible that they may really try to invent him. The truth is that multitudes of them would already accept the Pope if he were not called the Pope. I firmly believe that it would be quite possible, in this and many other matters, to play a sort of pious practical joke on large numbers of heretics and heathens. I fancy it would be quite feasible to describe in accurate but abstract terms the general idea of an office or obligation, which would exactly correspond to the position of the Papacy in history, and which would be accepted on ethical and social ground by numbers of Protestants and free-thinkers; until they discovered with a reaction of rage and astonishment that they had been entrapped into accepting the international arbitration of the Pope. Suppose somebody were to advance the old idea as if it were a new idea; suppose he were to say; "I propose that there be erected in some central city in the more civilised part of our civilisation the seat of a permanent official to represent peace and the basis of agreement among all the surrounding nations; let him be by the nature of his post set apart from them all and yet sworn to consider the rights and wrongs of all; Let him be put there as a judge to expound an ethical law and system of social relations; let him be of a certain type and training different from that which encourages the ordinary ambitions of military glory or even the ordinary attachments of tribal tradition; let him be protected by a special sentiment from the pressure of kings and princes; let him be sworn in a special manner to the consideration of men as men. " There are not a few already, and there will soon be many more, who would be perfectly capable of proposing such an ideal international institution on their own account; there are also many who would really, in their innocence, suppose that it had never been attempted before.

It is true that as yet large numbers of such social reformers would shrink from the idea of the institution being an individual. But even that prejudice is weakening under the wear and tear of real political experience. We may be attached, as many of us are, to the democratic ideal; but most of us have already realised that direct democracy, the only true democracy which satisfies a true democrat, is a thing applicable to some things and not others; and not applicable at all to a question such as this. The actual speaking voice of a vast international civilisation, or of a vast international religion, will not in any case be the actual articulate distinguishable voices or cries of all the millions of the faithful. It is not the people who would be the heirs of a dethroned Pope; it is some synod or bench of bishops. It is not an alternative between monarchy and democracy, but an alternative between monarchy and oligarchy. And, being myself one of the democratic idealists, I have not the faintest hesitation in my choice between the two latter forms of privilege. A monarch is a man; but an oligarchy is not men; it is a few men forming a group small enough to be insolent and large enough to be irresponsible. A man in the position of a Pope, unless he is literally mad, must be responsible. But aristocrats can always throw the responsibility on each other; and yet create a common and corporate society from which is shut out the very vision of the rest of the world. These are conclusions to which many people in the world are coming; and many who would still be much astonished and horrified to find where those conclusions lead. But the point here is that even if our civilisation does not rediscover the need of a Papacy, it is extremely likely that sooner or later it will try to supply the need of something like a Papacy; even if it tries to do it on its own account. That will be indeed an ironical situation. The modern world will have set up a new Anti-Pope, even if, as in Monsignor Benson's romance, the Anti-Pope has rather the character of an Antichrist.

The point is that men will attempt to put some sort of moral power out of the reach of material powers. It is the weakness of many worthy and well-meaning attempts at international justice just now, that the international council can hardly help being merely a microcosm or model of the world outside it, with all its little things and big things, including the things that are much too big. Suppose that in the international interchanges of the future some power, say Sweden, is felt to be disproportionate or problematical. If Sweden is powerful in Europe, she will be powerful in the council of Europe. If Sweden is too powerful in Europe, she will be too powerful in the council of Europe. And because she is the very thing that is irresistible, she is the very thing to be resisted; or at any rate to be restrained. I do not see how Europe can ever escape from that logical dilemma, except by discovering again an authority that is purely moral and is the recognised custodian of a morality. It may very reasonably be said that even those dedicated to that duty may not always practise what they profess. But the other rulers of the world are not even bound to profess it.

Again and again in history, especially in mediaeval history, the Papacy has intervened in the interests of peace and humanity; just as the greatest saints have thrown themselves between the swords and daggers of contending factions. But if there had been no Papacy and no saints and no Catholic Church at all, the world left to itself would certainly not have substituted social abstractions for theological creeds. As a whole, humanity has been far from humanitarian. If the world had been left to itself, let us say in the age of feudalism, all the decisions would have been rigidly and ruthlessly on the lines of feudalism. There was only one institution in that world that had existed before feudalism. There was only one institution which could possibly carry on some faint memory of the Republic and the Roman Law. If the world had been left to itself in the time of the Renaissance and the Italian statecraft of the Prince, it would have been arranged entirely in the current fashion of the glorification of princes. There was only one institution that could at any moment be moved to repeat, "Put not your trust in princes. " Had it been absent, the only result would have been that the famous settlement of CUJUS REGIO EJUS RELIGIO would have been all REGIO with precious little RELIGIO. And so, of course, our own day has its unconscious dogmas and its universal prejudices; and it needs a special, a sacred and what seems to many an inhuman separation to stand above them or to see beyond.

I know that this ideal has been abused like any other; I only say that even those who most denounce the reality will probably begin again to search for the ideal. But I do not, in fact, propose that any such spiritual tribunal should act like a legal tribunal or be given powers of practical interference with normal and national government. I am quite sure, for one thing, that it would never accept any such material entanglement. Nor do I, for that matter, desire that any of the secular tribunals now set up in the interests of international peace should thus have the power to interfere with nationality and local liberty. I would much rather give such power to a pope than to politicians and diplomatists of the sort to whom the world is giving it. But I do not want to give it to anybody and the authority in question does not want to accept it from anybody. The thing of which I speak is purely moral and cannot exist without a certain moral loyalty; it is a thing of atmosphere and even in a sense of affection. There is no space to describe here the manner in which such a general popular attachment grows up; but there is no doubt whatever that it did once grow up round such a religious centre of our civilisation; and that it is not likely to grow up again except for something which aims at a higher standard of humility and charity than the ordinary standard of the world. Men cannot have an affection for other people's emperors, or even for other people's politicians; they have sometimes been known to cool in affection even for their own politicians. I see no prospect of any such positive nucleus of amity except in some positive enthusiasm for something that moves the deepest parts of man's moral nature; something which can unite us not (as the prigs say) by being entirely international, but by being universally human. Men cannot agree about nothing any more than they can disagree about nothing. And anything wide enough to make such an agreement must itself be wider than the world.

THE SPIRIT OF CHRISTMAS

I HAVE rather rashly undertaken to write of the Spirit of Christmas; and it presents a preliminary difficulty about which I must be candid. People are very curious nowadays in their way of talking about "the spirit" of a thing. There is, for example, a particular sort of prig who is always lecturing us about having the spirit of true Christianity, apart from all names and forms. As far as I can make out, he means the very opposite of what he says. He means that we are to go on using the names "Christian" and "Christianity, " and so on, for something in which it is quite specially the spirit that is not Christian; something that is a sort of combination of the baseless optimism of an American atheist with the pacifism of a mild Hindoo. In the same way, we read a great deal about the Spirit of Christmas in modern journalism or commercialism; but it is really a reversal of the same kind. So far from preserving the essentials without the externals, it is rather preserving the externals where there cannot be the essentials. It means taking two mere material substances, like holly and mistletoe, and spreading them all over huge and homeless cosmopolitan hotels or round the Doric columns of impersonal clubs full of jaded and cynical old gentlemen; or in any other place where the actual spirit of Christmas is least likely to be. But there is also another way in which modern commercial complexity eats out the heart of the thing, while actually leaving the painted shell of it. And that is the much too elaborate system of dependence on buying and selling, and therefore on bustle and hustle; and the actual neglect of the new things that might be done by the old Christmas.

Normally, if anything were normal nowadays, it would seem a truism to say that Christmas has been a family festival. But it is now possible (as I have had the good or bad luck to discover) to earn a reputation for paradox simply by going on saying that truisms are true. In this case, of course, the reason, the only reasonable reason, was religious. It was concerned with a happy family because it was consecrated to the Holy Family. But it is perfectly true that many men saw the fact without specially feeling the reason. When we say the root was religious, we do not mean that Sam Weller was concentrated on theological values when he told the Fat Boy to "put a bit of Christmas, " into some object, probably edible. We do not mean that the Fat Boy had gone into a trance of mystical contemplation like a monk seeing a vision. We do not even mean that Bob Cratchit defended punch by saying he was only looking on the wine when it was yellow; or that Tiny Tim quoted Timothy. We only mean that they, including their author, would have confessed humbly and heartily that there was someone historically quite anterior to Mr. Scrooge, who might be called the Founder of the Feast. But in any case, whatever the reason, all would have agreed about the result. Mr. Wardle's feast centred in Mr. Wardle's family; and none the less because the romantic shadows of Mr. Winkle and Mr. Snodgrass threatened to break it up for the formation of other families.

The Christmas season is domestic; and for that reason most people now prepare for it by struggling in tramcars, standing in queues, rushing away in trains, crowding despairingly into tea-shops, and wondering when or whether they will ever get home. I do not know whether some of them disappear for ever in the toy department or simply lie down and die in the tea-rooms; but by the look of them, it is quite likely. Just before the great festival of the home the whole population seems to have become homeless. It is the supreme triumph of industrial civilisation that, in the huge cities which seem to have far too many houses, there is a hopeless shortage of housing. For a long time past great numbers of our poor have become practically nomadic. We even confess the fact; for we talk of some of them as Street Arabs. But this domestic institution, in its present ironical phase, has gone beyond such normal abnormality. The feast of the family turns the rich as well as the poor into vagabonds. They are so scattered over the bewildering labyrinth of our traffic and our trade, that they sometimes cannot even reach the tea-shop; it would be indelicate, of course, to mention the tavern. They have a difficulty in crowding into their hotels, let alone separating to reach their houses. I mean quite the reverse of irreverence when I say that their only point of resemblance to the archetypal Christmas family is that there is no room for them at the inn.

Now Christmas is built upon a beautiful and intentional paradox; that the birth of the homeless should be celebrated in every home. But the other sort of paradox is not intentional and is certainly not beautiful. It is bad enough that we cannot altogether disentangle the tragedy of poverty. It is bad enough that the birth of the homeless, celebrated at hearth and altar, should sometimes synchronise with the death of the homeless in workhouses and slums. But we need not rejoice in this universal restlessness brought upon rich and poor alike; and it seems to me that in this matter we need a reform of the modern Christmas.

I will now emit another brilliant flash of paradox by remarking that Christmas occurs in the winter. That is, it is not only a feast dedicated to domesticity, but it is one deliberately placed under the conditions in which it is most uncomfortable to rush about and most natural to stop at home. But under the complicated conditions of modern conventions and conveniences, there arises this more practical and much more unpleasant sort of paradox. People have to rush about for a few weeks, if it is only to stay at home for a few hours. Now the old and healthy idea of such winter festivals was this; that people being shut in and besieged by the weather were driven back on their own resources; or, in other words, had a chance of showing whether there was anything in them. It is not certain that the reputation of our most fashionable modern pleasure-seekers would survive the test. Some dreadful exposures would be made of some such brilliant society favourites, if they were cut off from the power of machinery and money. They are quite used to having everything done for them; and even when they go to the very latest American dances, it seems to be mostly the Negro musicians who dance. But anyhow, on the average of healthy humanity I believe the cutting off of all these mechanical connections would have a thoroughly enlivening and awakening effect. At present they are always accused of merely amusing themselves; but they are doing nothing so noble or worthy of their human dignity. Most of them by this time cannot amuse themselves; they are too used to being amused.

Christmas might be creative. We are told, even by those who praise it most, that it is chiefly valuable for keeping up ancient customs or old-fashioned games. It is indeed valuable for both those admirable purposes. But in the sense of which I am now speaking it might once more be possible to turn the truth the other way round. It is not so much old things as new things that a real Christmas might create. It might, for instance, create new games, if people were really driven to invent their own games. Most of the very old games began with the use of ordinary tools or furniture. So the very terms of tennis were founded on the framework of the old inn courtyard. So, it is said, the stumps in cricket were originally only the three legs of the milking-stool. Now we might invent new things of this kind, if we remembered who is the mother of invention. How pleasing it would be to start a game in which we scored so much for hitting the umbrella-stand or the dinner-wagon, or even the host and hostess; of course, with a missile of some soft material. Children who are lucky enough to be left alone in the nursery invent not only whole games, but whole dramas and life-stories of their own; they invent secret languages; they create imaginary families; they laboriously conduct family magazines. That is the sort of creative spirit that we want in the modern world; want both in the sense of desiring and in the sense of lacking it. If Christmas could become more domestic, instead of less, I believe there would be a vast increase in the real Christmas spirit; the spirit of the Child. But in indulging this dream we must once more invert the current convention into the form of a paradox. It is true in a sense that Christmas is the time at which the doors should be open. But I would have the doors shut at Christmas, or at least just before Christmas; and then the world shall see what we can do.

I cannot but remember, with something of a smile, that on an earlier and more controversial page of this book I have mentioned a lady who shuddered at the thought of the things perpetrated by my co-religionists behind closed doors. But my memory of it is mellowed by distance and the present subject, and I feel quite the reverse of controversial. I hope that lady, and all of her way of thinking, may also have the wisdom to close their doors; and discover that only when all the doors are closed the best thing will be found inside. If they are Puritans, whose religion is only based on the Bible, let it for once indeed be a Family Bible. If they are Pagans, who can accept nothing but the winter feast, let it at least be a family feast. The discordance or discomfort complained of by modern critics, in the family reunion, is not due to that mystical focal fire having been left burning, but to its having been left to go cold. It is because cold fragments of a once living thing are clumsily lumped together; it is no argument against making the thing alive. Christmas toys are incongruously dangled before heavy and heathen uncles who wish they were playing golf. But that does not alter the fact that they might become much brighter and more intelligent if they knew how to play with toys; and they are horrible bores about golf. Their dullness is only the last deadly product of the mechanical progress of organised and professional sports, in that rigid world of routine outside the home. When they were children, behind closed doors in the home, it is probable that nearly every one of them had day-dreams and unwritten dramas that belonged to them as much as Hamlet belonged to Shakespeare or Pickwick to Dickens. How much more thrilling it would be if Uncle Henry, instead of describing in detail all the strokes with which he ought to have got out of the bunker, were to say frankly that he had been on a voyage to the end of the world and had just caught the Great Sea-Serpent. How much more truly intellectual would be the conversation of Uncle William if, instead of telling us the point to which he had reduced his handicap, he could still say with conviction that he was King of the Kangaroo Islands, or Chief of the Rango Dango Redskins. These things, projected from within, were in almost all human spirits; and it is not normal that the inspiration of them should be so utterly crushed by the things without. Let it not be supposed for a moment that I also am among the tyrants of the earth, who would impose my own tastes, or force all the other children to play my own games. I have no disrespect for the game of golf; it is an admirable game. I have played it; or rather, I have played at it, which is generally regarded as the very opposite. By all means let the golfers golf and even the organisers organise, if their only conception of an organ is something like a barrel-organ. Let them play golf day after day; let them play golf for three hundred and sixty-four days, and nights as well, with balls dipped in luminous paint, to be pursued in the dark. But let there be one night when things grow luminous from within: and one day when men seek for all that is buried in themselves, and discover, where she is indeed hidden, behind locked gates and shuttered windows, and doors thrice barred and bolted, the spirit of liberty.

Lightning Source UK Ltd.
Milton Keynes UK
UKHW040649270619
345147UK00001B/114/P